WITHDRAWN
UTSA Libraries

The Theatre
of Goethe
and Schiller

Drama and Theatre Studies
GENERAL EDITOR: KENNETH RICHARDS
ADVISORY EDITOR: HUGH HUNT

Also in this series:

Theatre in the Age of Garrick
CECIL PRICE

A Short History of Scene Design in Great Britain
SYBIL ROSENFELD

The Theatre of Goethe and Schiller

JOHN PRUDHOE

ROWMAN AND LITTLEFIELD
Totowa, New Jersey

First published in the United States 1973
by Rowman and Littlefield, Totowa, New Jersey

ISBN – 0-87471-179-7

© Basil Blackwell, 1973

All Rights Reserved. No part of this publication may
be reproduced, stored in a retrieval system, or
transmitted, in any form or by any means, electronic,
mechanical, photocopying, recording or otherwise,
without the prior permission of Basil Blackwell & Mott
Limited.

All translations in this book are by the author. Those
from the final version of *Iphigenia in Tauris* and from
Wilhelm Tell are taken from the translations of those
plays published by Manchester University Press (New
York, Barnes & Noble), 1966 and 1970 respectively.

Library of Congress Cataloging in Publication Data
Prudhoe, John Edgar
    The theatre of Goethe and Schiller.

    (Drama and theatre studies)
    Bibliography: p.
    1.   Goethe, Johann Wolfgang von, 1749–1832—Criticism and
Interpretation. 2. Schiller, Johann Christoph Friedrich von,
1759–1805—Criticism and interpretation.
3. Theater—Germany—History.
I. Title. PT1964.P7 1973   832/6/09   73-1676
ISBN 0-87471-179-7

Printed in Great Britain

LIBRARY
University of Texas
At San Antonio

Author's Acknowledgements

I wish to thank Professor Ronald Peacock of Bedford College London, Professor Hugh Hunt and Mr. Kenneth Richards of Manchester University, and Mr. Colin Charlton, for reading the manuscript and for the many valuable criticisms and suggestions they have made.

JOHN PRUDHOE

Manchester, 1972

Contents

Illustrations

6. *Travelling Players in a Small Dutch Town.*
Oil painting by Gerrit Adrianse Berckheyde (d. 1698). (Bildarchiv der Österreichischen Nationalbibliothek)

7. *Pietas Victrix.*
Engraving by Gerard Boullats (?) of the performance at Vienna, 1659, showing scene of encampment and fortress. (Bildarchiv der Österreichischen Nationalbibliothek)

8. *The German clown Hanswurst in a 'Haupt-und Staatsaktion'.*
From Stranitzky's *Lustige Reyss-Beschreibung.* (Wiener Stadtbibliothek)

9. *Goethe as Orestes and Corona Schröter as Iphigenia in the Amateur Theatre production of* Iphigenia in Tauris.
Engraving by Facius (1805) after G. M. Kraus, 1779. (Nationale Forschungs-u. Gedenkstätten der klassischen deutschen Literatur in Weimar. Goethe-Nationalmuseum)

10. *Performance of* The Fisher Girl *in the park at Tiefurt.*
Water-colour by G. M. Kraus, 1782. (Nationale Forschungs-u. Gedenkstätten der klassischen deutschen Literatur in Weimar. Goethe-Nationalmuseum)

Between pages 118 and 119

11. *The Robbers* (Act IV, Sc. V).
Weimar, July 1811. Aquatint by J. C. E. Müller. (Theater-Museum, Munich)

12. *Gustaf Gründgens' Production of* Faust 1.
Deutsches Schauspielhaus, Hamburg. Will Quadflieg as Faust, Gustaf Gründgens as Mephisto. (Photo by Rosemarie Clausen, Hamburg 39, Gryphiusstrasse 5)

13. *The Conspiracy of Fiesco at Genoa* (Act V, Sc. XII). Weimar, May 1805. Aquatint by J. C. E. Müller after G. E. Opitz. (Theater-Museum, Munich)

Between pages 182 and 183

CHAPTER ONE

The Origins of Professional Theatre in Germany

Germany did not develop a native professional theatre until considerably later than many other Western European countries, largely owing to conflicts between the German-speaking states both during the Thirty Years War (1618–48) and long after. At the same time, however, she was under constant theatrical pressure from other countries whose touring companies found a ready welcome in her divided lands. It was not until 1767, only eight years before Goethe went to Weimar, that the first play of international importance with truly German characters and a German setting appeared—Lessing's *Minna von Barnhelm*. Thus it becomes impossible to assess the theatre of Goethe and Schiller without taking into account the influence of earlier foreign drama and the slow emergence of the German actor within its changing orbit. To consider this within a single chapter we shall concentrate on four aspects: (1) Amateur Theatre as it progressed from the Middle Ages to the Reformation, (2) Court Theatre under the Italian influence, (3) The English Comedians (*englische Komödianten*) who gave rise to the professional German touring players (*Wandertruppen*) and (4) The Theatre of Gottsched and Lessing.

Amateur Theatre

Amateur Theatre which had flourished in Germany, as elsewhere, under the auspices of the medieval Church, passed towards the middle of the fifteenth century into the hands of the Guilds. The best known of these Guilds is probably that of the Mastersingers whose dramatist Hans Sachs (1494–1576) appears in Wagner's opera and whose style Goethe echoes in parts of *Faust*. Sachs wrote several hundred folk comedies and though their four-beat doggerel makes no claim to literary pretensions, they have sufficient liveliness and naturalness of dialogue to make them still enjoyable. Many have become stock offerings of the puppet-theatre though originally written for live actors. The Mastersingers turned the *Marthakirche*, a Nuremberg church which had become disused as a result of the Reformation, into Germany's first permanent theatre building and here Sachs gave his actors some kind of training. Though they were amateurs (Sachs being a master cobbler) they were, as skilled tradesmen, accustomed to a system of apprenticeship and examination, and when in leisure hours they turned to poetry and music they naturally followed similar disciplines of instruction. Furthermore, as tradesmen, they were accounted respectable citizens. In these two respects—training and respectability—they were more favourably placed than the professional actors who followed them.

The precise features of Sachs's stage in the *Marthakirche* cannot be established, but it was certainly a simple construction. It was raised, had visible steps down to the audience at the sides, and steps hidden by a curtain at the back. The audience faced the platform, not being placed around three sides as in earlier practice. Perhaps this arrangement was suggested by the relationship of altar and congregation in a church, perhaps it was an imitation of the seating used for Latin plays presented by schools and universities at the time. Whatever the reason, it is clear that with his confined acting area and limited resources, Sachs could not imitate the Latin plays in another respect— their elaborate spectacle. Thus, even in the early years of the sixteenth century, the popular vernacular theatre of Germany was threatened by a more sumptuous, if learned, rival.

Something of a bridge between the learned and popular theatre was eventually established by School Plays devoted to religious propaganda and performed by Protestants and Catholics as a result of the Reformation. Yet this marriage of didacticism and entertainment was only partially successful, for instruction remained the chief aim. By the second half of the sixteenth century Jesuit schools began to present their scholars (sometimes augmented by professional singers) in entertainments combining religious teaching with great spectacle. At first such plays were in Latin and the representation of women on the stage, as well as their presence in the audience, was precluded. By the late sixteenth century, however, interludes and arias in German were allowed and the rules governing representation and presence of females relaxed. Jesuit plays with full German texts are extant from the end of the seventeenth century only. Even by the middle of the seventeenth century, however, German Jesuit plays included scenes of violence to appeal to popular taste—as is illustrated by a Graz play of 1640, where a doll figure of Jezebel was torn to pieces by dogs

Court Theatre

The Jesuit Theatre attracted the patronage and attention of the Catholic aristocracy and in some cases the local Jesuit school supplied the function of Court Theatre. Thus, in 1659 the Vienna college presented *Pietas Victrix*, an entertainment abounding in transformation scenes, the expenses for which were met by the Emperor. Protestant theatre was less lavish, but the plays of Andreas Gryphius (1616–64) show that he copied Jesuit methods. Like them he employed large casts, though his chief contribution to theatre was the advance he made in characterisation and linguistic style. He was a neoclassicist who conceived his tragedies on the models of France and the Netherlands. Had Germany, like Holland, succeeded in establishing a civic theatre by the third decade of the seventeenth century, Gryphius might have met with

3

greater success. Certainly he knew of the *Schouwburg* which Amsterdam had opened in 1638, and desired a similar enterprise in his own country. But Germany, when Gryphius returned from his foreign travels, was exhausted by war, whereas Amsterdam was a growing city rejoicing in new-found independence. It was also the home of the *Rederijkerkamers* (Societies of Rhetoric) which had a tradition for performing plays before they built their theatre and opened it with Joost van den Vondel's patriotic epic *Ghysbreght van Aemstel*. So while Vondel's plays became popular and were soon performed by Dutch companies who visited Germany, those of Gryphius found their only successful performances in schools. A subsequent attempt in the middle of the seventeenth century, by a professional English company, to perform them at Cologne and Frankfurt apparently met with little success.

Meanwhile German Courts had been invaded by Italian opera. The first performance of opera in German-speaking territory was at Hellbrunn, the pleasure palace of Marcus Sitticus Prince-Archbishop of Salzburg, in November 1618. It was probably performed by Italians, though singers from the Archbishop's own chapel may have been used. Professional Italian actors had been known in South Germany since 1496. These had been, however, chiefly troupes of acrobats and jugglers, forerunners of the kind of wandering company with which Mignon is engaged when we first meet her in Goethe's theatrical novel *Wilhelm Meister*. After them, about the middle of the sixteenth century, *commedia* troupes had arrived and become particularly popular in Vienna where, as the result of successive Emperors' marriages with Italian princesses, Italian was the language of the Court. From the second decade of the seventeenth century onwards Italian opera, with its attendant joys of stage machinery, became popular at many German courts and hence established a tradition for its performance which greatly affected the subsequent development of theatre. It is worth noting that machinery was introduced before opera itself. The first recorded performance at the *Steintheater* at

4

Hellbrunn was a play on St. Christina, some fifteen months before the opera mentioned above. Although the theatre was in the open air and possessed a natural rock stage, it was no part of Marcus Sitticus's intention to present a simple *al fresco* entertainment. Having studied in Italy, he determined to make his garden theatre (one of the oldest in Europe) as much like an Italian court theatre as possible. It seems likely that he hung the rocky walls with draperies and it is certain that he covered the stone stage with boards to support Italian *telari*: three-sided prisms which turned to give scenic variation.[1]

Once imported, Italian machines became ever more ambitious. In 1667, for the betrothal of the Austrian Emperor Leopold I with the Infanta of Spain, *La contesa dell'aria e dell' acqua* was staged in the inner courtyard of the Hofburg. It had one thousand three hundred performers, took several months to rehearse and included pageant cars with real fountains, dances, arias, lavish costumes and an equestrian ballet. At one end of the courtyard, so high that it overtopped the palace, was erected 'The Temple of Eternity'. This slowly descended from artificial clouds to the ground below and opened to reveal a Roman master of the horse, eight life-guardsmen, sixteen grooms and twelve trumpeters—all dressed in shining baroque armour with floor-length mantles and enormous plumes on their helmets. In their midst was the glittering figure of the Emperor, who then rode on his bejewelled horse towards his bride in the specially constructed Imperial-loge, thus initiating the spectacular equestrian climax of the performance.

Not all Courts could afford the lavishness of Vienna, but by 1696 the vogue for opera and machines had reached even tiny Weimar where a theatre was set up in the Wilhelmsburg for a performance entitled *Virtuous Love opposed by Vicious Desire*. This is some forty years before we can trace the presence of professional actors at the Weimar Court, for the love of music did not necessarily betoken desire to encourage wandering

[1] See Heinz Kindermann, *Theatergeschichte Europas* (Otto Müller Verlag, Salzburg). vol. III (1959), p. 485.

players. Indeed, Duke Ernst August of Weimar (1688–1748) is characterised as much by his love of the first as his hatred of the second, and he issued several edicts banning wandering actors from his domains. (Perhaps, in early years, he made an exception of Johann Friedrich Lorenz, whose company advertised themselves at Hamburg in 1738 as 'Weimar Court Comedians', but their authority for doing so cannot be established. If their claim was justified, they would be the first professional company connected with the Duchy.)

Rise of Professional Actors in Germany

From the middle ages until Goethe's time the professional actor, be he acrobat or even, like Johannes Velten (1640–?92), university graduate, was socially unacceptable. To this was sometimes added ecclesiastical disfavour. When Velten played at Berlin and sought to receive Holy Communion, he was refused entry to the church and when, as a dying man in Hamburg, he again requested the Sacrament it was again denied him. Much the same attitude on the social level is shown by Melina's father and stepmother in *Wilhelm Meister*, when they discover she has run off with an actor and order the young couple to be arrested and tried. Such isolated incidents as the raising of the Italian comedian Cechini to the aristocracy, by Kaiser Mathias of Austria in 1613, do not detract from this generally unfavourable picture. Rather does the surprise and disbelief which Mathias's action caused, emphasise it the more. And though the actors in *Wilhelm Meister* claim that their profession is coming to be held in higher repute, we must set against this the author's wry comment in Book III, Chapter viii:

The entire company of actors was also frequently commanded to present itself in front of the nobility, especially after dinner had been concluded. This they regarded as the greatest honour and failed to observe that at precisely the same hour it was customary to have the huntsmen and servants bring in a pack of hounds, and to have the horses paraded in the castle courtyard.

6   The salvation of the professional actor from the late sixteenth

century to the eighteenth lay in a noble patron who was interested in his art. The first professional actors to visit Germany came by ducal invitation. They were an English company, headed by William Kempe, who crossed to the continent in the retinue of the Earl of Leicester when he went to assist the Dutch against Philip of Spain. Leicester sent his actors with a letter of recommendation to the Court of Frederick II of Denmark. So great was their success that Frederick's nephew, Christian I of Saxony, requested their presence at his own court. At first Kempe was unwilling to make the journey, being daunted, perhaps, by the language barrier. He demanded the high salary of 100 Thalers a year for his troupe and, when this was eventually agreed to, arrived at Weidenhain in September 1585. He remained there three months, the terms of his employment requiring his company to perform at all Court festivities by singing, playing instruments, acrobatics and the performance of plays with music.

Kempe's success encouraged others. In 1592 Robert Browne (previously an actor with Alleyn in England) took a troupe to the Netherlands and Germany, bringing with them a letter of recommendation from Lord Howard and visiting the Court of another relative of Frederick of Denmark, that of his son-in-law, Heinrich Julius of Brunswick. (Heinrich Julius was so impressed that he eventually turned author of several plays, based on English models.) When Browne's company left the Brunswick Court they gave public performances at the Frankfurt-am-Main Autumn Fair of 1592, including the plays of Marlowe and *Gammer Gurton's Needle* in their repertoire. Neither the 'mighty line' of the first, nor the word play of the second were comprehensible to the audience, however, and when Browne returned to Frankfurt twelve months later he presented Biblical plays whose stories were well known and could be helped out by music and mime.

Browne's company, and many others who followed them until the later years of the sixteenth century, only survived in Germany by remembering that actions spoke louder than

7

B

words. Stress had to be laid on visual elements such as jigs, clowning, murders, duels and executions. Eventually the English Comedians learned German, using it at first only for interludes and subsequently for the entire performance. The date of the completion of this linguistic change cannot be exactly fixed, but probably Browne's actors were playing in German by 1600. It was not a literary German, but a patchwork of colloquialisms and the officialese they learned from court functionaries, but as long as it communicated bare facts to the audience its purpose was fulfilled. In the process of introducing German into their plays, English companies found it useful to recruit native actors, who thus became the first German professional players. The Germans were first used principally as stop-gaps between scenes. Such, for example, was the function of the 'roguish clown' recorded at Münster in 1601, who kept the audience amused while his English colleagues changed costumes. Gradually more German actors joined the English troupes, so that by the time George Jolly, the last of the *englische Komödianten*, returned home at the Restoration all-German troupes of wandering actors had emerged. The success of the English companies had been so great, however, that many of these new German *Wandertruppen* continued to style themselves 'English Comedians' in their publicity.

The nature of *Komödianten* performances changed considerably between 1585 and the 1650s. The early period suggests that actors mostly relied on their own memories in reassembling texts. When Green's troupe returned to Germany in 1626, however (war having forced him home in 1620,) he seems to have taken original English role scripts with him. Since he had already worked in Germany for between fifteen and twenty years the translations of these texts were more accurate and flexible than those used in the first quarter of the century, though still far below the literary standard of their English originals. Staging, too, was gradually modified. Inevitably the wandering actors had to adapt themselves to any conditions that were to hand, whether at Court or in the market-place, but

8

by 1654 George Jolly's company had acquired an Italianate winged stage and actresses for female parts. These, in fact, were the first German actresses. Previously women had only appeared in Italian troupes and it was probably competition from the Italians while he was touring in Vienna, Strassburg and Basel, that induced Jolly to make these changes.

Whatever the changes, however, visual effects and clowning remained of paramount importance. Actors were given bladders of blood to lend verisimilitude to scenes of horror and figures like Spencer's 'Hans Stockfisch', Sackville's 'Jan Bouschet' and Reynolds' 'Pickelherring' delighted audiences with broken-German humour. The introduction of German dialogue gave some clowns opportunity for greater coarseness and hence the actors incurred the displeasure of the more puritanical. It is not surprising, therefore, that in 1606, Browne protested to the Frankfurt council that

. . . no-one shall be offended by our play, but rather everyone given opportunity to see himself reflected there, to recall his own weaknesses . . . and to learn to pursue Decency and Virtue.[2]

The *Wandertruppen* who emerged from the *englische Komödianten* continued to perform plays from the old repertoire. Probably the most famous of their texts is *Der bestrafte Brudermord (Fratricide Punished)* with its alternative title *Prince Hamlet of Denmark*. This was published in 1781 from a manuscript possessed by the actor Conrad Ekhof. Originally, however, the play was in the repertoire of Carl Andreas Paulsen whose company came into prominence in the 1660s. Possibly it was presented in some form or other even earlier than this, for Green's company gave *A Tragedy of Hamlet, a Prince in Denmark* at Dresden in 1626. The relationship of Paulsen's text to Green's cannot be established, nor can we answer the vexed question of the relationship of Paulsen's version to Shakespeare's. But a glance at the *Brudermord* reveals a good deal about the German professional theatre some eighty years before Goethe's birth.

[2] Heinz Kindermann, *op. cit.*, vol. III (1959), p. 356.

In the title *Fratricide Punished or Prince Hamlet of Denmark* the baldly stated moral is given priority over the chief figure. In the same way a company presenting *The Tragedy of Lear, King of England* in 1666 adopted a cumbersome title to explain that it was 'a play in which the disobedience of children towards their parents becomes punished, their obedience, however, rewarded'. Such crude morality was held more important than poetry or psychology. Of verse in the *Brudermord* there is none— unless we include the first twenty lines of an irrelevant prologue which must have been added late in the period since they require the appearance of Night 'in a starry machine'. Perhaps the entire prologue (in which Night instructs the Furies to sow discord between the King and Queen of Denmark—an aspect of the plot which comes to nothing) was merely borrowed from another entertainment for specific occasions. Whatever its purpose, it reveals the typical *Wandertruppen* desire to produce the theatrically effective regardless of style and logical consequence. The same disregard for unity of style occurs when the Ghost is allowed to box the ear of a soldier, and when the mad Ophelia makes love to the Court Fool, Phantasmo. Though several lines suggest Shakespeare's original, six of the seven great soliloquies are missing and the total playing time reduced to under an hour. A clownish peasant, Jens, is introduced and in Act IV, Sc. I we follow Hamlet to an island that presumably lies between Denmark and England. His companions (shadowy relatives, perhaps, of Rosencrantz and Guildenstern) are two bandits who announce their intention to kill him. The Prince begs time to pray and says he will raise his hands when ready. 'Shoot now' he calls and the stage direction goes on:

He falls down forwards between the two bandits who shoot and kill each other.

—a theatrical, if unconvincing, way of reminding the audience that crime does not pay! Further stress on visual effects is illustrated by the stage directions for the duel between Hamlet and Leonhardus (Laertes):

Leonhardus lets the rapier fall and seizes the poisoned épée which lies ready. He stabs the Prince en carte in the arm. Hamlet parries Leonhardus so that both drop their weapons. Each runs to his rapier. Hamlet gets hold of the poisoned épée and stabs Leonhardus dead.

Goethe's *Wilhelm Meister* reveals that the wandering actors of the next century were also highly skilled in fencing.

In addition to English plays the professional actors of the seventeeth century began to perform versions of such foreign masters as Molière and Calderon. They also evolved a style of improvised drama known as *Haupt- und Staatsaktionen*—plays dealing with intrigue in high places. The effects of this were felt even at the time when Schiller's *Don Carlos* was given its second production at Leipzig in 1787. Here the actor playing King Philip, Brückl by name, had been trained to play tyrants in *Haupt- und Staatsaktionen* and accordingly improvised freely. Whenever he delivered a line that struck him as particularly significant he admonished the audience to 'Take note of that!' (*Merkt Euch das!*)—a proceeding which did not endear him to the author.

Connected with the *Haupt- und Staatsaktionen* was the figure of *Hanswurst* (John Sausage) who owed something to English clowns like *Pickelherring* and something to the Commedia figure of *Arlecchino*. At the same time he was unmistakably German, or, to be more precise, in origin Austrian. Created by Josef Anton Stranitzky (1676-1726) he made his debut in Vienna where, as we have seen, Commedia troupes were popular at Court. Hanswurst, however, appealed to the people rather than their rulers. Even when Stranitzky had become popular in the newly built *Theater am Kärntnertor*, the Imperial Court ignored him and invited only Italian players. But Hanswurst's popularity spread throughout German-speaking lands, where Stranitzky's red jacket, neck-ruff, yellow trousers, pointed green hat and peasant braces were imitated by many other actors. In his broad leather belt he carried a wooden sword (derived from Arlecchino's bat) and his hair was gathered into a comic bun on the top of his head. Originally his accent was that of a

11

Salzburg peasant and his function was to blunder through the scenes of the play duplicating serious action on a comic level. When the young lover begged leave to kiss the feet of his royal mistress, Hanswurst would sue to kiss her garters and promptly start to raise her skirts in order to do so. Yet, as Professor Kindermann has rightly insisted,[3] such buffoonery did not satirise the serious action, it merely provided a comic counterpart. In the hands of less gifted men than Stranitzky, Hanswurst became coarse, and indeed, the whole genre of *Haupt-und Staatsaktionen* degenerated into self-indulgent chaos.

Unfortunately the actors lacked the imagination and education to raise themselves from this situation. From the Courts, dominated by Italian opera, no help or guidance was forthcoming. The actors, therefore, contented themselves with pleasing the vulgar, indulging their own whim for virtuoso roles and taking no heed of the higher aspects of their profession. That the same attitudes persisted into the eighteenth century can be seen from Goethe's description of Wilhelm Meister's first contacts with the actors (*Wilhelm Meister's Apprentice Years, Book I, Ch. xv*):

Totally occupied with frivolity, they seemed to think of their profession and their aim least of all things. He never heard them discuss the poetic worth of a play, nor judge it rightly or wrongly. It was always simply a question of what the play would make. Is it a play that will draw? How long will it play? How often can it be given again? And other questions and observations of the same nature. Then they usually turned on the manager, declaring he was too parsimonious with wages and that he was especially unfair to this or that individual. Then they blamed the audience for seldom rewarding the right man with applause. They declared the German theatre was daily improving itself, that the actor was honoured more and more according to his worth and that he could not be honoured enough. They also spoke a great deal of coffee-houses and wine-gardens and of what went on in such places. What debts this or the other colleague had contracted and how much money he must suffer to be deducted from his earnings as a result. They complained

12   [3] See Heinz Kindermann, *op. cit.*, vol. III (1959), pp. 560 ff.

of inequalities in the weekly payment and of intrigues amongst their opposite numbers. But in the end it always came back to a discussion of the great and well-deserved attention which the audience paid to them—in which the influence of the theatre on the education of both a nation and the world at large was not forgotten.

This picture of trivial interests mixed with self-congratulation must, of course, be set against the callowness of Wilhelm in the first part of the book. There is a double point being made. Not only were actors like this, but Meister is naïve to be surprised at the fact. He was equally innocent to be shocked by the disorder in an actress's apartment, but in those days

... how happy did he rate the actor whom he saw in possession of so many fine clothes, suits of armour and weapons, and who constantly practised a form of behaviour whose spirit seemed to mirror the noblest and finest circumstances, opinions and passions which the world had manifested. In like manner Wilhelm had pictured to himself the home life of an actor as a series of noble actions and concerns, of which the theatrical representation was the outward and visible climax. It had seemed to him like a piece of silver that had long been held in the furnace of the refiner's fire and finally shone in full beauty to the eyes of the workman, indicating to him at the same time that the metal had now been cleansed of all foreign additions.

How greatly, therefore, he was startled at first when he visited his beloved and looked through the mists of happiness which surrounded him to behold the tables, chairs and floor. The debris of transient, insubstantial and vain ornament lay scattered in wild disorder about the room like the glittering armour of a newly-scaled fish. The very tools of human cleanliness—her combs, soap, towels, still bearing traces of the uses to which they had been put,—were not concealed from view. Music, play-scripts of her roles, shoes, washing and Italian flowers, etuis, hair-pins, pots of make-up and ribbons, books and straw-hats, none of these was suffered to scorn the neighbourhood of the other and all were united by the common element of dust and powder. (*Ibid.*)

Wiser men than Wilhelm had long known that behind the glitter of the stage lay chaos, not only in the dressing-room but in the actors' minds. One by one foreign traditions had been haphazardly adopted. To that of the English Comedians were added those of the *commedia* and the theatre of machines. In the seventeenth century Dutch touring companies brought the neo-classicism of Vondel together with elaborate mimed interludes in lavish costume. French and Spanish plays were also imported, though, of course, heavily adapted. The total result was an unedifying, inartistic confusion. Actors might still speak as Browne had done of the stage as a means of teaching men 'to pursue Decency and Virtue', but where was the art and imagination to put such a mission into practice?

Gottsched, the Neubers and Lessing

Only if we recall the disordered history of German theatre can we understand why reformers like Gottsched and Goethe seem to have been dictatorial. Only despotism could save the situation. Goethe was, in general, a benevolent despot and though his fore-runner Johann Christoph Gottsched (1700–66) is an easy target for anti-academic abuse, without him Weimar theatre would not have been possible.

Gottsched, a lecturer at Leipzig University, was a rationalist who saw in French neo-classicism, as formulated by Boileau, the only hope for German theatre. As an academic he was unwelcome to actors, but he realised that reform could only come through players who worked under his influence rather than through pamphlets penned in his study. In Caroline Neuber (1697–1760) and her husband, Johann, he found two actors whose backgrounds allowed them to respect his ideals. Johann, least gifted of the pair, had studied jurisprudence; Caroline, before she took a characteristically venturesome jump through a window to elope with her husband, had received a good grounding in French and Latin at home. Both were dissatisfied with the state of German theatre before they met Gottsched at the Leipzig fair of 1727. Caroline, generally known as *Die Neuberin* (*The* Frau Neuber)—the definite article prefixed to her name indicating her importance as theatrical manager—immediately allied herself to Gottsched and proceeded to perform his translations of French drama. Her style of acting these was based on that of French companies who visited German courts at the beginning of the eighteenth century. Unfortunately this style was already outmoded in France, representing not the more naturalistic acting of Molière's time but the bombastic manner of the earlier Versailles' period. The language of both Gottsched's translations and his original play *The Dying Cato* were equally remote from everyday life.

Caesar: Then Cato, shall I now speak gentle Mercy's word?
Or how shall I lay hand on sharp Revenge's sword?
What is the Senate's wish?
Cato (*passionately*): What your still threatening breath
Has wished upon them all! Descent from power! Or death!
War and war alone can grant us victory
And none of us prize life where freedom cannot be.
(Act IV, Sc. III)

Gottsched's precepts, set forth in his *Attempt at a Critical Art of Poetry for the Germans* (1740), were as inflexible as his stage rhetoric. Concerning the Unity of Place we read:

The spectators remain sitting in one place and it follows that the persons taking part in the play must also remain all in one location which the spectators may look upon without changing their position.

This application of perverse logic to stage illusion is coupled with a strong sense of bourgeois morality, so that in turning to the Unity of Time he recommends that the action be confined as far as possible to three or four hours, but that 'these hours must be in the day-time not in the night, for the night is intended for sleeping'. The prime aim of the dramatist was to inculcate morality: he was to start with 'a moral principle' and form around it 'a fable through which the truth of such a principle may be illuminated'. Thereafter he should search the pages of history to discover personages whose adventures most closely fitted his invented story, thus lending prestige and versimilitude

15

to the whole. But he need not stick to history too closely, particularly if the supernatural were involved for that was an offence against reason. Comic interludes too—in particular those of Hanswurst—were regarded by Gottsched as the gravest offence against cultured taste. But with the banning of comedy went also such nearness to life as the German stage possessed. Prose was replaced by alexandrines and the actor, hitherto reliant on improvisation, found himself bound by an intractable text and forced to adopt the bombastic posturings it implied.

Frau Neuber followed these precepts as far as she was able, but she was also a shrewd theatrical manager who knew she could not live by Gottsched alone. Furthermore she delighted in 'breeches parts' and roles which gave opportunity for numerous disguises. She therefore also included in her repertory *Haupt- und Staatsaktionen* and other remnants of the earlier theatre. Even her famous Leipzig performance of 1737, when Hanswurst was tried on stage for his misdemeanours and banned from the German theatre for ever, is ambiguous. If inspired by Gottsched's theories, it also owed something to practical necessity, for she was then suffering competition from Joseph Müller's immensely popular, if coarse, Hanswurst performances. There was therefore theatrical cunning as well as idealism in bringing the clown on to her own stage, letting him have his fun, and finally delighting the audience by burning a doll in his likeness. That the attempt to banish Hanswurst failed is also worth noting. He reappeared in other companies and was used by Goethe for his entertainment *The Fair at Plundersweilen* (staged by the Weimar Amateur Theatre in 1778), where he speaks in dialect, wears his traditional costume and interrupts the play-within-the play

> Which is the history
> Of Esther in a Mystery,
> But told in modern kind
> With shudders and horrors combined.

16   He outlasted even Goethe's half-loving mockery of *Haupt- und*

Staatsaktion on this occasion, for his present-day successor is Kasperl, the glove puppet of children's theatre. Thus it will be seen that the reforms of Gottsched and Frau Neuber were only partially successful. Nor, unfortunately, were some of his most enlightened ideas adopted by her—those concerning costume. Gottsched wanted Greek and Roman plays performed in classical costume, Neuber usually acted them in the wigs and dress of Versailles.

Eventually Gottsched and Frau Neuber quarrelled and he then worked with two former members of her troupe, Heinrich Koch (1703–75) and Johann Schönemann (1704–82). Koch's company, still somewhat influenced by the Gottsched tradition, was performing in Leipzig when Goethe was a student there from 1765–8. Not surprisingly the young law student was critical of their performances, although his violent reaction to the 'Theatre of Rules' was only in the first stages of its formation. But he was well acquainted with the works of Gottsched's most distinguished critic, Gotthold Ephraim Lessing (1729–81) and appeared at this time as an amateur actor in a production of *Minna von Barnhelm*.

After the quarrel with Gottsched, Caroline Neuber befriended the young Lessing and performed his early plays, which were light comedies in the French manner. His later work was to show the influence of England rather than France, and not only did he translate Dryden's *Essay of Dramatic Poesy*, but produced in 1755 a tragedy *Miss Sara Sampson* which owed much to the English Sentimentalists. This play and the later *Emilia Galotti* (1772) laid the foundation for such subsequent bourgeois tragedies as Goethe's *Clavigo* and Schiller's *Intrigue and Love*. In all Lessing's major plays we find elements which the Weimar dramatists were to take up. In *Minna von Barnhelm* (1767) the scenes between Minna and Franziska recall those of Portia and Nerissa and perhaps the incident of the ring (pawned by Tellheim and unknown to him returned to his beloved Minna, who proceeds to cure his Prussian pride with Portia-like stratagems) owes something to the same Shakespearean source. Certainly if Lessing had not championed the cause of Shakespeare so vigorously in his critical writings, the subsequent influence of the English poet in Germany might have been less. The combined English influence of Shakespeare and Richardson on Lessing's own drama, however, did not prevent his establishing a natural German style of speech. It is this which gives his dramas life, despite the fact that the plots are too symmetrically designed and were labelled by a Romantic critic 'dramatic algebra'. This criticism was originally made of *Emilia Galotti*, a reconstruction of the Appius and Virginius story, in which a middle-class father stabs his daughter to death rather than surrender her to the lust of a prince. But the stricture applies even more to *Nathan the Wise* (first performed 1783). Here the fable of Nathan's adopted daughter Recha, brought up a Jewess, who falls in love with a Christian Knight-Templar and eventually proves to be his lost sister (while both eventually discover the Knight-Templar's Mohammedan captor to be their uncle) is clearly designed as religious allegory rather than realistic drama. Despite this *Nathan* remains one of the most powerful and haunting works of the eighteenth century. One cannot ignore either the subtle touches of characterisation in Nathan, or (more importantly) the breadth of Lessing's own vision. In the twentieth century the Christian Churches are beginning to consider reunion, in the eighteenth Lessing pointed out that ultimate Truth lay beyond the imagery of any particular sect and might be approached equally well through the symbolism of any. The most famous scene of the play is that in which the Saladin, the Knight-Templar's Mohammedan captor, sends for Nathan, the wise Jew, and is told the parable of the rings. A certain family, says Nathan, possessed the Ring of Truth which had the power of making its possessor loved by all men. It was passed in each generation to the son whom a father loved most. In one generation, however, the father loved three sons equally well and accordingly gave each a ring without revealing which was genuine. On the father's death the sons quarrelled and went to a judge to settle

18

their differences. The judge, on hearing that the true ring made its possessor loved by God and man, declares that all three rings must be false. It is clear that each brother loves only himself. He advises them to mend their quarrel and to love each other, in order that the power of the ring may be regained though the original is lost. This type of religious thought, together with the distrust of the absolute value of symbols which it implied, was to exercise profound influence on the Weimar stage.

As a critic, Lessing is of even greater international importance than as a dramatist and here, too, his influence on Goethe and Schiller is considerable. His essay *Laokoon or the Frontiers of Pictorial Art and Poetry* (1766) points out that while pictorial art is static and must confine itself to the portrayal of beauty, descriptive art (including drama) follows an action from beginning to end and may include elements of ugliness not proper to painting or sculpture. He sees drama as 'transitory painting' and this realisation that it contains both pictorial and literary elements was to bear fruit in the stress which Goethe and Schiller placed on grouping, lighting, scenery and movement.

Most important of Lessing's critical works is the *Hamburg Dramaturgy*, written during his association with the Hamburg National Theatre (1767–8). This first German National Theatre was founded by twelve citizens of Hamburg who invited Lessing to be its official critic and literary adviser—its *Dramaturg*. Although the Hamburg Enterprise quickly failed through mismanagement, public apathy and lack of suitable plays, it gave an example which others were to follow and left behind it in the *Hamburg Dramaturgy* a body of criticism which, as Allardyce Nicoll observes 'is worthy almost of being placed alongside Aristotle's *Poetics*'.[4] Taking up the Aristotelian concept of Purgation, Lessing insists that Gottsched and earlier German critics had mistranslated the Greek as speaking of 'Pity and Terror' (*Mitleid und Schrecken*), whereas a true translation is

[4] A. Nicoll, *World Drama* (Harrap, London, 1949), p. 414.

'Pity and Fear' (*Furcht*). The fear which Aristotle refers to, he goes on

. . . is most certainly not the fear which the evil threatening another awakens in us *for that person*, but rather the fear which arises in ourselves from our likeness to the one who suffers. It is the fear that the misfortunes which we see hanging over him could afflict us. It is the fear that we ourselves might be the subject for pity.

Thus he concludes that Pity and Fear must be roused simultaneously in the spectator. The function of tragedy is not, as Gottsched had supposed, to teach moral precepts, but rather to stimulate moral and intellectual awareness in the spectator by his sharing the suffering of the protagonist. Gottsched's rationalism is replaced by an approach of refined sensibility in Lessing. For him even the form of drama is to be dictated by the rules which the subject itself implies:

. . . The true judge of art does not deduce rules from his taste, but has formulated his taste according to the rules which the nature of the matter demands.

He does not, therefore, advocate lawlessness in drama as the *Sturm und Drang* dramatists were to do. Having banished the dogmas of French neo-classicism, he enthrones the discipline of cultivated feeling and instinct. Form is organic, not imposed, just as the style of acting introduced at Hamburg by Lessing's friend and collaborator Conrad Ekhof (1720–78) was both naturalistic yet at the same time highly disciplined.

Ekhof had joined the Schönemann company in 1739, where he had acted roles in the Gottsched tradition, but his natural genius, together with slight physical deformity, resulted in his developing a more personal style. In 1750 the Schönemann troupe was invited to the Court of Schwerin in Mecklenburg and here, three years later, Ekhof, who was for practical purposes now the head of the company, had founded the first Academy of Acting in Europe. Its aims were to indicate the actor's standing as a 'professional' man and to examine critically the nature of his art. It proceeded by lectures, discussions and play readings to set standards not only for the Schönemann company (whose attendance was voluntary) but for German theatre as a whole. Ekhof opened the first meeting of his Academy with the words:

Let us, therefore, ladies and gentlemen, study the grammar of acting—if I may term it so—and make ourselves better acquainted with the means we must employ if we are to become capable of looking into the cause and motivation of all things, so that we neither speak nor act anything without sufficiently understanding its basis and cause, and so that we may be worthy of the name of Artists.[5]

Through a study of Aaron Hill's *On the Art of Acting*, he learned of the naturalness which Garrick had brought to the contemporary English stage. He insisted that the actor's business was:

... to imitate Nature through Art, to come so near to Nature that appearance must be taken for reality and that things which have already occurred are represented as though they were now occurring for the first time.[6]

In a later session he turned to Francesco Riccoboni's *Art of the Theatre* (which Lessing had translated) and laid particular stress on the words:

If we draw no attention to our outward appearance and the spectator believes he sees nothing but the working of our soul, then, indeed, the nobility of art is at its zenith.[7]

The words foreshadow Goethe's later theories, just as Ekhof's insistence on play readings before rehearsals began foreshadow later Weimar practice. Since the actors were given only partial scripts containing the relevant cues and their own lines (a practice incidentally still to be found in the typescripts of older plays and operettas hired out to British amateur societies in

[5] Quoted by Joseph Gregor, *Weltgeschichte des Theaters* (Phaidon-Verlag, Zürich, 1933), p. 489.
[6] Quoted by Kindermann, *op. cit.*, vol. IV (1961), p. 514.
[7] Kindermann, *ibid.*, p. 515.

the twentieth century) it was essential to hold such readings to make the continuity of action apparent to all concerned. But Ekhof went further than this. He referred to the practice as 'Concerting the action' and endeavoured to make clear to each player the significance of his role in the pattern of the play.

The joint presence of Lessing and Ekhof in the 'Hamburg Enterprise', then, contributed much to Weimar theory and practice. Ekhof was later to act in Weimar, as we shall see, and later still, when at Gotha, to take into his company the young August Wilhelm Iffland (1759–1814), whose subsequent productions of Schiller's plays at the beginning of the nineteenth century contributed so greatly to making the poet popular throughout Germany.

CHAPTER TWO

Goethe's Early Plays

Johann Wolfgang Goethe was born on 28 August 1749 at Frankfurt-am-Main, the son of middle-class parentage. His paternal grandfather had been a tailor and subsequently an inn-keeper, and his father was an Imperial Councillor in Frankfurt. His mother, twenty years her husband's junior, was the daughter of the town's chief magistrate. She was eighteen years old when the poet, her first child, was born and the relationship between them was extremely close. Of five other children only the second, Cornelia, survived to maturity and for her Goethe felt something of the devotion which is reflected in his play *Brother and Sister (Die Geschwister)*.

Apart from a brief period at school while the family house was being rebuilt in 1754 the boy's early education was private, some of the best teachers in Frankfurt being engaged to instruct him. His father, a somewhat stern and forbidding man, possessed a fine library and had lived for a time in Italy. From him the boy learned his early lessons in German and Latin, and by the time he was eight was already writing exercises in German, French, Latin, Italian and Greek. His imaginative faculty was meanwhile stimulated by the fairytales his mother told him, always being careful to allow the child to contribute his own ideas to their development. The breadth and energy of Goethe's mind, which was later to be equally at home in the fields of science and the arts, were thus early manifested and

23

developed. Even his characteristic mixture of religious faith and scepticism was illustrated in early youth, for the Lisbon earthquake which occurred in 1755 roused his first doubts as to the paternal nature of God. At the age of sixteen he was sent to Leipzig University as a student of Law and subsequently transferred his studies to Strassburg in 1770.

Goethe's interest in theatre was awakened when he was about three or four years old by the gift from his paternal grandmother of a puppet-theatre, still preserved in the birth-house in Frankfurt. This present, he reports in his autobiography *Poetry and Truth*, 'made a particularly strong impression on the boy' and held a special place in the children's affection since its donor died soon after. When some four years later the Seven Years War came to Frankfurt and it was necessary to keep the children more at home than hitherto, the theatre was much used and provided the young Wolfgang with his first experience as a 'director'. Perhaps memories of the chequer-board floor of the toy stage prompted his later theory (*Rules for Actors*, 1803) that the actor should imagine the stage to be 'a kind of draughtboard' when deciding on his movements. Certainly his interest in his own theatre would have been further stimulated by visits of professional puppeteers to the town at fair time, and from them he may well have gained his first introduction to a Faust play.

During the Seven Years War, French troops occupied Frankfurt bringing with them actors to entertain the officers. A free pass to the entertainments was sent to Goethe's maternal grandfather, Chief Magistrate of the town:

I had received a free ticket from my grandfather, which I used daily, contrary to the wishes of my father but with my mother's support. Here I sat, then, in the stalls of a foreign theatre and paid all the more attention to movement, mime and expression of speech, since I understood little or nothing of what was spoken up there on the stage and therefore derived my entertainment from gestures and voice alone. I understood least of the comedies, because they were spoken quickly and concerned themselves with affairs of every-day life, the expressions for which were totally unknown to me. Tragedy was performed less often and the measured pace, the rhythm of the Alexandrines and the universality of the language made this in every sense more comprehensible to me. It was not long before I took down the Racine which I found in my father's library and declaimed the plays with great vivacity, for they had impressed themselves both on my ear and the so closely related organ of my speech, though I could not at that time have understood the continuity of a single passage. But I learned whole speeches by heart and recited them like a well-schooled parrot—a process made all the easier to me by the fact that as a child I had been accustomed to memorise sections of scripture, which were for the most part beyond my understanding, and to recite them in the manner of the Protestant preachers.   (*Poetry and Truth*, Book III)

These early theatre visits taught the boy to appreciate and imitate the outward theatricality of the stage, though we notice his ability to reproduce cadences of the human voice had manifested itself even earlier as a result of church-going. It was an ability which was later to serve him well as a dramatic poet. Goethe's stage verse is always admirably designed for speaking aloud: he hears the actor as he writes. This quality has unfortunately not been preserved in many English translations and hence an important aspect of his drama is unknown to non-German readers. As will be shown later, part of the success of plays like *Iphigenia* and *Faust* on the stage is the extraordinary naturalness of the dialogue, and allowance for the requirements of the actor, within formally structured verse.

The French actors' presence in Frankfurt allowed Goethe to become friendly with one of their company, a boy whom he calls Derones in his autobiography. It was to this young critic he submitted the manuscript of an early play, of which he confesses he could remember little in his old age except that 'the scene was rustic and had no lack of princesses, kings and Gods'. He recalled clearly, however, his friend's reactions and the lessons they taught:

Derones read through the play attentively and as he sat down with me to alter a few details, he turned the entire piece upside down so that no stone was left resting on another. He crossed out, he put back, removed one character, substituted another—in short went to work in the maddest and most arbitrary way possible until my very hair stood on end. I was predisposed to believe he must understand such matters for he had told me so much of the three Unities of Aristotle, the regularity of the French stage, probability of theatrical happening, harmony of verse and all that goes with it, that I was forced to suppose him not only educated in such matters but deeply grounded in them. He ran down the English and despised the Germans—in short he recited the entire litany of rules for dramatic composition which I have had to hear repeated so many times in my life.   (*Ibid.*)

As a result of his conversations with Derones, Goethe turned to the critical essays of Corneille and Racine, the latter soon becoming his god among playwrights. The critical writings of the French, however, he found less awe inspiring:

But through all this I became more confused than before, and after I had tortured myself for some time with this chop-logic, this theoretical prattling from the past century, I threw out the baby with the bathwater. I cast aside the whole trumpery business with greater confidence, the more apparent it became to me that these authors themselves, who had brought forth such magnificent things, when once they began to discuss their works, to give grounds for their actions, to defend and excuse themselves, were equally sometimes at a loss to hit the nail squarely on the head.   (*Ibid.*)

Yet he grew up in a world still influenced by French theatre and at sixteen appeared in an amateur performance of Racine's *Britannicus*. When a student at Leipzig University he attempted a translation of Corneille's *Le Menteur* and his original plays of this period reveal the influence of Molière. If he had doubts as to the validity of French theory, the French neo-classical manner influenced his style.

'A Lover's Humour' and 'Partners in Guilt'

These two plays from the Leipzig period, though slight, deserve attention both for the sense of stage-craft they exhibit and the light they throw on Goethe's later dramatic method. Since neither these, nor subsequent short plays performed by the Weimar Amateur Theatre, are easily available in English translation, the quotations here provided from them are longer than their position in the canon of Goethe's work might otherwise warrant.

Like so much of Goethe's writing *A Lover's Humour* is based on personal experience, being a dramatic representation of aspects of his love affair with Anna Katharina Schönkopf (Aennchen), daughter of a Leipzig wine merchant. Of this episode in his life Goethe later observed:

Through my groundless and preposterous jealousies I ruined the happiest days both for her and for myself.

In the play the pastoral hero, Eridon, is aptly described as one

Who since he knows no care invents care for himself.

Jealousy makes him forbid his doting mistress Amina to attend a feast, until her friend Egla resolves to teach him a lesson. This scene reveals sure and sophisticated dramatic technique, and though the stage directions may have been added later than the original version, we cannot doubt that the dramatist visualised something of what they indicate at its inception. The use of triple rhyme, when Eridon succumbs to Egla's wiles, is an effective way of stressing the climax and foreshadows the method of later dramas, in which variation of rhythm and rhyme scheme frequently points development of character and action.

Eridon: If only I could bear
      To watch the many hands that touch hers in the dance!
      See other eyes on hers and see them gain her glance—
      The very thought of that divides my heart with spite.
Egla: Let such things take their course. Their substance is so
        slight.
      A kiss, itself, is nothing.   27

Eridon: What? Nothing in a kiss?

Egla: I'm sure a heart must feel a great deal more than this
Before it speaks at all. But will you not forgive?
For if you treat her ill, what hope has she to live
Happily?

Eridon: My dear friend . . .

Egla (*flattering him*): Dear friend, be wise and good.
Farewell!

(*She takes his hand.*)
Your hand is hot.

Eridon: The pulsing of my blood. . . .

Egla: Still angry, then? Enough. I see that she's forgiven.
I'll go to her at once, where she beseeches heaven
To let her know your whim, and tell her all is well.
Her heart will calm its course: her love for you will swell.

(*Looks at him tenderly.*)
Take care! She'll seek you out when revelries have ceased,
And by that search itself her love will be increased.

(*Egla acts more and more tenderly towards him, leaning on his shoulder.
He takes her hand and kisses it.*)
At last she sees you there! O, what a moment, then!
You seize her, feel yourself the happiest of men.
Dance makes the fair more fair, the blushing cheek more
red,
A mouth that smiling breathes—soft curls drop from the
head
Around the panting breast. A gentle charm enhances
The grace of every limb that to the music dances,
Veins glow more deep and full, and as the body sways
The quickening fire of life sets every nerve ablaze!

(*Egla affects to be tenderly moved and sinks her head on his chest. He puts
his arm around her.*)
The pleasure of that sight—what joy can be its peer?
Yet you forsake the dance and shun all feeling here.

Eridon: O, friend, here at your breast, my feeling is too near!

(*He falls on Egla's neck and kisses her. She allows him to do so, then takes
several steps backs and asks flippantly*)

28 Do you love Amina?

Eridon: Yes. . . . . . .

. . . .

        If sweet Amina's kiss brings me such heavenly joys,
        May I not feel the same in one brief kiss of yours?
Egla: *That* you must ask yourself.

The pastoral convention enables Goethe to present his own experience in a non-realistic setting. Within an apparently literary form he makes us feel the pulse of life, or rather of certain isolated aspects of life, and in this we may perceive the seeds of his later dramatic technique.

Partners in Guilt shows the same awareness of stage business and close relationship of words to actions. Goethe's avowed master here was Molière, but the influence of German writers like Weisse and Krüger is pointed out by some critics, and the inquisitive landlord perhaps owes something to the inn-keeper in *Minna von Barnhelm*. The Landlord's daughter, Sophie, is married to the wastrel Söller but agrees to a secret assignation with her former admirer, Alcest. Söller overhears their meeting since he has come to the room to rob Alcest and this central scene is described by G. H. Lewes as being 'like the whole of the play . . . a mixture of the ludicrous and the painful—very dramatic and very unpleasant'.[1] Lamb, one feels, would have been more tolerant towards it, pointing out, as he did when confronted with the 'immorality' of Restoration Comedy, that the characters 'have got out of Christendom into the land . . . of cuckoldry, where pleasure is duty, and the manners perfect freedom'. None of the four characters is admirable (the Landlord is a busybody prepared to betray his own daughter, Sophie is a flirt, Alcest only too willing to accommodate her and Söller is a thief and gambler) but they excuse themselves by wit, the artificiality of the Alexandrine convention and the liveliness of the action:

[1] See Lewes, *Life of Goethe* (Everyman Edition), p. 51.

Act Two: Scene Four

ALCEST *fully dressed with hat and sword, wearing a cloak which he immediately puts aside.* SOPHIE *and* SÖLLER.

[Söller is concealed in an alcove, his presence unknown to the others]

Alcest: Have you been waiting long?
Sophie: Sophie was first, my dear.
Alcest: You're trembling?
Sophie: I'm afraid.
Alcest: My darling!
Söller: Darling! Dear! So starts the masquerade!
Sophie: You know too well the pain my heart once bore for you.
          You know that heart completely and will pardon what I do.
Alcest: Sophie!
Sophie: If you forgive my heart, I'll feel no sin.
Söller: You'd better ask me first if I'll forgive you *him*!
Sophie: What brought me here tonight? I vow I hardly know.
Söller: I'd hazard a shrewd guess.
Sophie: It's like a dream.
Söller: So! So!
          I wish it *were* a dream.
Sophie: The weight of my distress
          Is all that I can bring you.
Alcest: Complaint makes suffering less.
Sophie: Only with you can I find sympathy forever.
Söller: You'd call it sympathy if you shared a yawn together!

. . . .

Sophie: My husband can't conceive how rational creatures live.
          When I think how much I've *said*! How much ground I
             give!
          He tipples all day long. He runs up endless debts.
          He stinks, he dices, brags! Gambles! Panders! Bets!
          The children of his brain?—Tomfooleries! Flat jokes!
          For him the soul of wit lies in some country hoax.
          He lies, traduces cheats . . .

Söller: I see she has the gist
          Of the sermon for my funeral gathered in that list.

The stage direction near the end of the scene reveals that per-haps even in his student days Goethe sought the kind of picturesque grouping that was to be characteristic of Weimar classicism in later years:

Exit SOPHIE. ALCEST accompanies her through the centre door which remains open so that we see them standing together in the distance.

In the wit of the rhyming couplets we also detect something of the later style—not only the wit of Mephistopheles in the scenes of *Faust I*, which were written before Goethe went to Weimar in 1775, but his sallies in the scenes that were added later in Rome, and his characteristic cynicism in certain scenes of Part II. For this reason it is wrong to draw too sharp a line between Goethe's early dramas and his later ones. Both *A Lover's Humour* and *Partners in Guilt* show neo-classical influence. Soon Goethe was to reject 'The Theatre of Rules', but that rejection was only temporary. New rules, more congenial to his own Romantic spirit, were sought and eventually formulated. When he left Leipzig (owing to illness) and subsequently transferred his University studies to Strassburg in 1700, he came under influences that led to the writing of his *Sturm und Drang* tragedy *Götz von Berlichingen*. It is in many ways the least characteristic of his plays, and it is the only one of his major dramas that can justly be described as formless. Even *Faust*, though its total construction is episodic and somewhat arbitrary, has a demon-strable over-all pattern. Goethe's genius naturally sought form in the theatre, from his early admiration of Racine to his final composition of *Faust II*. His experiences in Strassburg and the opinions he held there were a temporary forsaking of this instinctive search, a turning-away which allowed him to turn back and see essentials more clearly.

Götz von Berlichingen

Among Goethe's Strassburg friends was Johann Friedrich

Herder, a poet and critic some five years his senior, who persuaded him to re-read Homer and make serious study of Rousseau, Ossian, Goldsmith and Shakespeare. His admiration for the last—and indeed his whole attitude when writing *Götz von Berlichingen*—may be judged from the *Shakespeare Address* which he gave to a literary society in Strassburg, which contains the famous words:

I did not for one moment hesitate to abandon the Theatre of Rules. The Unity of Place seemed to me so terrifying an imprisonment, the Unities of Action and Time such burdensome fetters to our imaginative powers! I sprang forth into the free air and only then did I feel I had hands and feet.

His admiration for Shakespeare was also strengthened by the influence of another friend, Lenz, the dramatist whose *Observations on the Theatre* (1774) embody the dramatic credo of the *Sturm und Drang* (Storm and Stress) movement.

For Lenz and the adherents of *Sturm und Drang*, (the movement is called after a play by Klinger with the same title, 1775), Shakespeare's sublimity lay in his supposed disregard of rules. Modern drama, Lenz held, with characteristic revolutionary thoroughness, must take 'a different point of departure from that of Aristotle'. The modern dramatist must start with a consideration of the 'popular taste . . . of our fatherland, which still remains the popular taste of today and will always remain so'. Thus an appeal to the growing feeling of nationhood among the German States colours his whole thought. Greek audiences, he held, had gathered to see a single action, modern German audiences were interested rather in a single hero. They were not interested in 'the secret influences of inexorable Fate', but rather in the majestic romanticism of a great man. Accordingly the unity of plot is swept away, all that is required being a series of episodes illustrating the main figure and 'following each other like thunderclaps'.

Many of Lenz's theories are exemplified in *Götz von Berlichingen* and help us to understand its enormous popularity with the reading public when published in 1773. Goethe borrowed his material for the play from the autobiography of a robber knight who lived 1480–1562. By turning him into a kind of Robin Hood figure 'whom the princes hate and to whom the oppressed may turn', he created a national hero whose appeal to the audiences of his own country is comparable to that of Shakespeare's Henry V in England. Moreover, he supplied him with a language that was fresh, vernacular and exciting. Here, for the first time since Shakespeare, was the use of dramatic language which ranged from the coarse expressions of the soldier's camp to the heights of poetic rhetoric. Götz can invite an Imperial Captain to lick his arse as naturally as he later speaks of 'trees putting forth their buds and all the world alive with hope'. The power and variety of language in the play has always been one of its main attractions. In 1799 it was translated (not entirely successfully) by Sir Walter Scott and contributed to the line of historical romance pursued in the Waverley novels. In the 1960s an adaptation of it, which retains its linguistic power far better, was made by John Arden and produced at the Bristol Old Vic.

Almost as successful as his use of language, is Goethe's handling of the vast historical background against which his hero stands. Historically, Götz was important as the champion of *Faustrecht*—the law of survival of the fittest which had permitted knights of the Holy Roman Empire (a loose alliance of German-speaking States under an elected Emperor) to wage predatory wars against each other. At the Diet of Worms (1521) the Emperor Maximilian abolished *Faustrecht*, a decision welcomed by the Bishops and Princes as a means of strengthening their power. To men like Götz, however, for whom plunder was a way of life, its abolition seemed an intolerable infringement of their ancient freedom. Accordingly they allied themselves with the peasantry in common struggle against spiritual and temporal despotism.

This historical situation seemed to the German followers of Rousseau to reflect their own condition and attitudes in the

33

eighteenth century. In Goethe's play, Götz becomes a 'noble savage' in sixteenth-century armour, while the corruption of the Bishop of Bamberg's court reflects both the general evil presumed to be inevitable in 'civilisation', and the particular rottenness contemporary radical thought detected in the German Courts of its own time. Thus the history is brought alive on the stage. In Act I, Sc II, for example, we have a memorable glimpse of the Lutheranism of the sixteenth century seen through the eyes of Goethe's own day. Götz meets Brother Martin whose name and vocation suggest those of the Protestant rebel. In place of a wearisome and undramatic discussion of the theology behind the Reformation, Goethe presents a vivid scene in which the Monk complains of the 'unnaturalness' of his vow of chastity and breaks his fast by drinking the health of Götz's wife, adding as he does so 'I know no women—and yet woman was the crown of creation'. A similar happy parallel between the two centuries is drawn in the scene between Götz and his son Carl, where the parrotlike learning of the later age is amusingly satirised. Carl recites his lesson 'Jaxthausen is a village and castle on the Jaxt' without realising that his father is master of that castle. Götz's comment that he, himself, had known 'every path, track and ford' of the surrounding country before he knew their names, speedily establishes his own Rousseauistic romantic stature.

History is also brought alive by the engaging mixture of warmth, idealism and bluntness in the hero's character. His generosity and tenderness are illustrated in Act I when he captures Weislingen, now the Bishop of Bamberg's man, but formerly Götz's friend, and recalls their boyhood days:

Götz: ... We two always stood together. Everyone knew us for that. (*Pours wine and brings it.*) Castor and Pollux! It did my heart good when the Margrave called us that.

Weislingen: The Bishop of Würzburg gave us the name.

Götz: And a learned man he was! A warm heart too. I'll never forget him as long as I live. Used to put his arm round us and declare it was wonderful the way we understood each other—

say how lucky a man was to have a twin-brother as his companion.

Weislingen: No more of that!

Götz: Why not? When work's over, there's nothing pleasanter than recalling days gone by. Oh, I admit that when I think of it— how we went through thick and thin together and were everything to each other—I say to myself as I used to 'All our days ought to be like that!' Wasn't that my only consolation when my hand was shot off at Landshut and you looked after me? You did more for me than any brother. I hoped that Adalbert von Weislingen would be my right hand from then on. But now . . . (Act I, Sc. III)

This passage is in Goethe's mature manner, foreshadowing a similar recollection of youthful friendship between Orestes and Pylades in *Iphigenia*. The historical reference to the loss of Götz's hand is naturally and economically made, and the emotions of the hero lyrically transformed from the particular to the universal level.

In the same way, Götz's idealism throughout the play arises naturally from the historical situation. He is shown as loyal to the Emperor, only quarrelling with the corruption of the Empire:

. . . I'm no rebel. I've committed no offence against the Emperor. As for the Empire—it's no concern of mine. . . . When have I raised a finger against the House of Austria? Haven't all my actions always proved I'm more aware than any man what Germany owes to her ruler? Especially what the little men, the Knights and freemen owe to their ruler. (Act IV, Sc. II)

He not only dies with the cry of 'Freedom' on his lips, his whole manner bespeaks freedom when he is captured and brought to trial for insurrection. He confronts his judges with a forthright common sense which recalls such figures as Webster's Vittoria Corombona and Shaw's St. Joan:

Götz: Good morning, gentlemen. What do you want with me?

Councillor: First that you consider where you are and before whom you stand.

35

Götz: I give you my oath that I do not mistake you for people you
are not.

. . . .

Councillor: Sit down.
Götz: Down there? I can stand. That little stool smells too much
of poor sinners—just like the whole room.
Councillor: Very well, then. Stand.
Götz: Let's come to the point please.
Councillor: We shall proceed according to law and order.
Götz: I'm glad to hear it. I wish you'd done so earlier.   (*Ibid.*)

Goethe's intention was, undoubtedly, to make Götz more
than this figure of infectious courage, warm-heartedness and
blunt rebellion. He intended to make him a tragic figure by
showing, in the second half of the play, how his idealism was
betrayed by the ruthlessness of his allies, the peasants. In this,
however, he is not so successful as in the earlier scenes. The later
scenes exhibit not so much a conflict of idealism versus ruthlessness, as a conflict of styles. Scenes such as those between Götz
and Weislingen, Götz and Brother Martin, and Götz and Carl
approach realism. The peasant leaders, however, especially in
the first version of the play *The History of Gottfried von Berlichingen
with the Iron Hand dramatised* (1771) are presented in scenes of
Sturm und Drang fantasy. It is not merely that they themselves
are lacking in pity, fear and idealism, the language they are
given to speak seems to preclude such things by its own exaggerated convention. Asked, for example, whether his aristocratic
prisoners shall be killed next day, one of the peasant leaders,
Metzler, replies:

Tomorrow? No, today. It is already passed midnight. See how the
mountains around us are bathed in the reflection of light like glowing blood from their castles. O sun, arise! Arise! When your first
broken ray dawns red and joins with the fearful glitter of the flames,
we will lead them out. We shall stand before them with blood red
faces and our pikes shall tap their blood from a hundred wounds.
Not their blood! Ours! These leeches shall give back our blood
again. Let no man aim at their hearts. They shall bleed to death.

36

And if I saw them bleed a hundred years, my revenge would not be
sated.   (*History of Gottfried von Berlichingen*, Act V, Sc. II)

At Herder's suggestion, Goethe modified such passages in the
second version which was published in 1773, but their basic
tone still remained. For this reason we cannot accept Götz
as a satisfactory tragic figure—though he remains a fascinating
romantic hero. The forces which cause his downfall do not seem
to belong to the world in which we have witnessed his most
admirable qualities and hence we cannot take them as seriously
as we take the hero himself.

All Götz's enemies (with the exception of Adelheid, who does
not really have anything to do with him in the play) lack the
life that is in him. Bamberg is well drawn but quickly fades
from the scene. Weislingen is colourless, though he is to some
extent a self-portrait of the author. Goethe's greatest difficulty
in writing the play was that the facts of Götz's life—a series of
petty wars which left him to die unspectacularly of old age —
did not provide sufficient material for a drama. The theme of
romantic rebellion was there, but little else. The poet had,
therefore, to invent the complicated and sprawling intrigue for
himself, and partly did so by translating his own experience into
dramatic fable. While at Strassburg he had fallen in love with
Friederike Brion, daughter of a parson in the near-by village
of Sesenheim. Eventually he realised that she could not be his
ideal marriage partner and deserted her, though the parting
caused him considerable heart-searching. Out of his remorse
grew the figure of Weislingen in this play as well as certain aspects of Clavigo and Faust later. Of the three figures only Faust
is a success: Weislingen is reduced to characterless interjections
in his scenes with Götz and becomes a lay figure in the Adelheid
episodes. Reconciled to Götz at the start of the play, he is
betrothed to Götz's sister Maria. He quickly returns to the
Bishop of Bamberg's court, however, and the charms of
Adelheid von Walldorf, who eventually tires of him and kills
him.   37

In the first version of the play Adelheid's villainy goes far beyond this. She seduces not only Wesilingen but also Maria's eventual husband, von Sickingen. Having been condemned by the *Vehmgericht* (a secret tribunal of justice) for her crimes, she even seduces the man sent to murder her, traitorously stabbing him to death in her bedroom. In the 1773 version this melodramatic scene was cut and the whole intrigue surrounding Adelheid considerably simplified. Here we are left with a character who provides excellent opportunities for flamboyant acting, many of whose scenes, though somewhat literary in inspiration, show touches of realism akin to that which is used in Götz's portrait. Her words to her waiting-woman, after her parting from Weislingen in Act II, Sc. VI, though they recall Cleopatra's ability to be 'quickly ill, and well' are an example of Goethe's true observation of her character:

See me again? I'll answer for it, he will. Margarete, when he comes, turn him away. I'm ill! I have a headache—I'm asleep! Anything! Turn him away. If there's a means to win him, this is it.

Götz was first produced by Koch in Berlin in 1774, a stage adaptation being made by Karl Lessing, younger brother of the author of *Nathan the Wise*. The production was as revolutionary as the text. Brückner, in the leading part, discarded the French wigs normally used for tragic heroes in Frederick the Great's theatre, and played in his own hair. An attempt was made to achieve 'historical' costumes throughout. The result was an overwhelming success, although the author's name was left off the playbill for the first performance, appearing thereafter as 'Herr D. Göde from Frankfurt-am-Main'.

Six months later it was staged by Schröder at Hamburg in his own adaptation. Considerably abridged and with the order of scenes transposed, it was nearer to the original than the Berlin performance. Fearful of the success of so unconventionally constructed a piece, Schröder presented it only after having first put on the more conventional *Clavigo*. His strategy was only partially successful: *Clavigo* ran seven nights and

Götz only four. Subsequently it was performed with success in many other German cities and has since remained one of the most popular of all Goethe's plays. The version prepared by him for Weimar and performed in two parts (*Adalbert von Weislingen* and *Götz von Berlichingen with the Iron Hand*) in 1819 represents an attempt to re-order the youthful impetuousness of the play in terms of his later classicism. This third version lacks the power of the original, however. The second, 1773, version has become the standard text for the theatre.

Clavigo

The subject of Goethe's next play was suggested by the *Mémoires* of Beaumarchais, author of the *Marriage of Figaro*. The events in it had happened only ten years before Goethe wrote the play (1774) and illustrate, therefore, a significant attempt to set a tragedy in contemporary time. The play was hastily written and for that reason, perhaps, has been discredited by some critics. It is, however, of importance in tracing Goethe's development as a dramatist and contains scenes of great interest.

Out of the historical Clavigo (José Clavijo y Fajardo, 1730–1806, a Spanish journalist and secretary to the Cabinet of Natural History) he creates a more imposing literary figure, one, in fact, nearer to himself. Goethe's Clavigo has 'strength of thought' and 'burgeoning imagination' we are told by his friend Carlos, and he unites the two with 'brilliance and lightness of style'. He also resembles his author in being, like Weislingen, an untrue lover.

Clavigo has courted Marie Beaumarchais for six years and then deserted her. Her brother arrives from France to demand satisfaction, forcing Clavigo to sign a confession of his betrayal. Clavigo and Marie are reconciled until Carlos persuades him that to marry her would be to betray his literary destiny. Tortured by this second desertion, Marie dies of a broken heart. Clavigo fights a duel with Beaumarchais over her coffin and is

39

mortally wounded, at the same time forgiving his foe and requesting that he be brought safely across the frontier.

The ending of the play, though melodramatic in the *Sturm und Drang* manner, is often held to foreshadow the kind of reconciliation which is characteristic of later Goethean tragedy. In production, however, this is scarcely discernible, for such an interpretation rests on a few lines of the dying Clavigo only. The real significance of the play as a contribution to European drama lies in the earlier scenes—those between Carlos and Clavigo where we find a use of debate on the stage which preludes the work of Ibsen and Shaw.

Carlos, Clavigo's friend and confidant, stands out as a modern figure, a Goethean counterpart to Shaw's Tanner in *Man and Superman*. In some ways he is closer to Don Juan than Shaw's reconstruction of him—like Juan he is a self-confessed womaniser—but he is also a clear-thinking philosopher who sees through the cant of bourgeois morality. He analyses Clavigo's dilemma with masterly logic. 'There are few men,' he points out, 'who are at the same time so brilliant and industrious as you.' 'You came from home without any income —so much the better. It should have made you the more eager to gain a living and the more careful how you maintain it.' He is willing to allow any man his romantic follies, but insists that wise men know that life is made of sterner stuff. He says of Marie:

She is poor and has no position. If Clavigo had not had his little affair with her, no-one would know she even existed. They say she's well-bred, pleasant, witty! Who's going to marry a woman for that? All that fades in the first weeks of marriage. O, says someone, people say she's beautiful. Quite exceptionally beautiful and charming.—Why then, I understand, says someone else. . . .

(Act IV, Sc. I)

Carlos argues as Goethe must have argued with himself at the time of leaving Friederike Brion. Yet, as we have said, Clavigo is also a self-portrait and hence the author's figure is split into

40

two opposites. The result is a drama of debate preluding similar confrontation of opposites in later plays: Egmont and Alba, Iphigenia and Pylades, Tasso and Antonio, Faust and Mephistopheles. Only Götz, among Goethe's major stage heroes, lacks this opposite figure. The Bishop of Bamberg is his *enemy*, but his role is small and the two never meet on stage: they do not share a common crisis which each views in a different way. The Carlos–Clavigo scenes, therefore, mark a significant point in Goethe's development as a dramatist. They suggest Shaw in method as well as thought—they concern themselves with opinions rather than facts or even, in the conventional sense, characters. Carlos, for example, is known to us only by the way he thinks. He does practically nothing in the play. Yet critics have sometimes seen him as the villain of the piece. The reason for this is the weakness of Clavigo:

> Carlos, I am not a great man. . . . Make me able to act and I will. I have no thought of my own. Think for me.   (*Ibid.*)

The apparatus of debate having been set up, one of the speakers proves wanting. It was not till later that Goethe learned how to give both significant weight. But Carlos is far from a villain. He is the advocate of common sense who sees that beauty must fade and marriage be a union of souls. His arguments are anti-romantic but not unscrupulous:

> We don't lack greatness when circumstances force us to act, but only when they overwhelm us. Take another breath and you'll be yourself again. . . . You've long ago paid back what that poor girl did for you. And as for saying you're in debt to her for her first reception of you, why, any woman would have done as much, and more, for the pleasure of your company, without making such pretensions! And would it, by any chance, ever occur to you to give your old schoolmaster half your income because he taught you your A B C thirty years ago? Would it, Clavigo?   (*Ibid.*)

In the first three acts of the play the background of stiff Spanish etiquette (an easy target for *Sturm und Drang* social criticism) lends cogency to Carlos's views. Even the scene in

41

which Beaumarchais forces Clavigo to sign his declaration in the presence of the servants (though sometimes criticised as melodramatic) worked admirably in the production brought by the Schiller Theater to London in 1965, the liveried and expressionless flunkeys placed by the free-standing windows at the side of the stage, symbolising the rigid convention that threatened Clavigo's freedom. The *Sturm und Drang* protest is contained within the framework of an ordered plot, and sensitive production such as this stressed the unity of the whole. While not one of Goethe's greatest plays, *Clavigo* proves itself eminently actable, and the rejection of the loose construction of *Götz* is an important indication of the direction of his future work.

Stella

The first version of *Stella* was written in 1775, a subsequent revision with a different ending for the Weimar stage being published in 1816.

The basic plot of both versions is the same. Cäcilie Sommer brings her daughter, Lucie, to be companion to Stella, a baroness whom she has never met. From the local postmistress, Cäcilie learns that the baron (Fernando) has deserted Stella, and that her daughter died soon after birth. Fernando, it is hinted, was a man 'of curious principles—leastways he never came to church', but he was well respected by the country people and devoted to Stella.

Then suddenly we heard that his Lordship was gone. Gone away and never came back.

Cäcilie observes in an aside that this is a reflection of her own fate also. When Fernando enters later we learn that he has in fact deserted both women. Having married Cäcilie he left her for Stella, having subsequently repented his act he had sought for his wife again. Believing Cäcilie to be dead, therefore, he now returns to Stella once more.

In the original version of the play the dilemma is finally

solved by a *ménage à trois*, a solution in keeping with the moral freedom advocated by *Sturm und Drang* thought. In the version performed at Weimar in 1806, a more conventional ending was supplied: Stella takes poison and Fernando shoots himself. The attempt to turn the play into a tragedy, however, is a failure, for the early scenes do not prepare us for such a conclusion. The strength of the play lies in its lyrical language and its moments of sensitive insight into character. Though the first ending is sensational it cannot, in context, be considered immoral, the atmosphere of the whole being too rarified and idyllic to admit questions of moral realism.

Cäcilie and Stella are contrasted characters who immediately become friends. Cäcilie, the older, is the more worldly wise who, despite her own misfortunes, respects the idealism that Stella retains after Fernando has deserted her. 'You carry heaven in your heart' she tells Stella. 'You are happy! In spite of everything you still live in the deepest, purest feelings of humanity' (Act II). The word 'humanity' (*Menscheit*) is the key to her character. It occurs again in her speech to Fernando in Act V, Sc. II when she outlines the possibility of three lovers cohabiting. Though she is not a fully developed character, Cäcilie's high-mindedness, generosity and warmth of feeling are arresting. Against her Stella is more impulsive and inexperienced. It is she who makes the first proposal of friendship which proved so susceptible to ridicule by critics of the play:

Madame! An idea has suddenly come to me. We shall be to one another what our husbands should have been. We will share this house together.—Your hand! From this moment on I will never leave you.   (Act II)

Against the basic story-line of the play Stella's words seem sentimental and unconvincing. But in the text they are followed by Stella's account of her own daughter's death, a passage that immediately lifts us into a world where such idealism seems possible. Here the economy of expression delineating deep human suffering points directly to Goethe's later style: 43

She lay before me! The bud was plucked! And I stood—my inmost heart turned to stone.—There was no pain! No consciousness—I stood!—Then one of my women picked the child up, pressed it to her heart and suddenly said 'She's still alive!' I fell on her, put my arms round her neck—my tears fell in thousands on the child— down before her feet—But she'd deceived me. She lay dead and I beside her in wild, hideous despair.   (*Ibid.*)

The starkness of the description, its lack of all irrelevant circumstantial details, presents experience of grief which we recognise as universal. This, we feel, is the essence of bereavement not merely the description of a particular death. Such passages of universal experience lead naturally to the universalised idealism of the final scenes. When Cäcilie reveals her final vision of the nature of love we recognise it as something we would all aspire to, if only our natures were not mortal. She tells Fernando:

I reproach you with nothing. . . . Up till now I bemoaned your loss, I pined because of things I could not alter. Now I have found you again and your presence gives me new life, new strength. Fernando, I feel that my love for you isn't selfish, not the passion of a lover who would give everything to possess the object she desires. My heart is warm and full for you, Fernando. It is the feeling of a wife who is prepared to sacrifice even her own love for the sake of love itself.   (Act V, Sc II)

Such sentiments represent the extreme idealism of *Sturm und Drang* but are presented in terms of debate rather than melodrama. In *Clavigo* the debate comes first and the play ends with histrionics that fail to represent the serious core of the piece. In *Stella* the final crisis *is* the debate, and the idealism which is Goethe's main concern finds appropriate expression at the climax of the dramatic action. Thus the play marks a step forward in his dramatic technique. At the same time, it must be admitted that as in *Clavigo*, the debate is one-sided. Fernando, like Goethe's previous unfaithful lovers, remains a shadow. All the light glows from Cäcilie as she develops her ideal of

'Humanity'. She seems almost to include the other two chief characters in herself: Stella, one feels, will one day develop into a Cäcilie, and Fernando (at least in the first version) is moulded by her opinions as Clavigo is by Carlos's.

The dominance of Cäcilie in the closing scene finally reduces the debate to a 'set piece' like Nathan's fable of the rings, or Flamineo's tale of the crocodile in *The White Devil* and the Duchess of Malfi's tale of the salmon. Cäcilie tells the tale of a Crusader who was saved from death by his captor's daughter. The girl eventually returns home with him to his wife and is presented to her. The wife realises that she owes her husband's life to his new mistress, and that he had followed the demands of 'Humanity' in bringing her with him after she had risked everything to save his life. Love must be rewarded with love: in its purest form it must not admit sexual jealously. Thus, Cäcilie tells Fernando, the wife in her story told the girl:

Take everything that I can give you. Take half of what already belongs to you completely. Take all of him. And leave me all of him. Each of us shall have him yet rob the other of nothing.

(Act V, Sc. II)

As in all fairy-stories the ending is happy: God in Heaven rejoices in this display of selfless love and blesses them.

The language of *Stella* is more controlled than that of the earlier plays, the economy and near-poetic quality of much of the prose enabling us to accept the idealism of the thought, undisturbed by the jarring influence of realism. But the Weimar ending destroys the poetic idealism by returning us abruptly to the world of shotguns, conventional morality and sudden death. Goethe made the alteration because in his maturity the ideals of *Sturm und Drang* were no longer acceptable to him. Moreover the play had always been regarded as extremely shocking. The production by Schröder in Hamburg in 1776 was banned after only two performances by order of the Senate. The Weimar version, was, however, well received and since it

45

is included in the Collected Works has hitherto tended to be the one most used subsequently in Germany. In the late forties of the present century, however, an excellent production of the first version was mounted in Vienna with Käthe Dorsch as Cäcilie and Käthe Gold as Stella.

CHAPTER THREE

Schiller's *Sturm und Drang* Dramas

Schiller was born ten years later than Goethe, on 10 November 1759 at Marbach in Württemberg, the son of an army surgeon. When he was seven the family moved to Ludwigsburg, residence of Duke Karl Eugen of Württemberg, and here the boy had his first glimpse of the Court life which he was later to portray so memorably on the stage. Here, too, inevitably, he first tasted the joys of Italian opera, and from these early impressions sprang perhaps much of the essential style of his subsequent theatre. Childhood theatricals in the garden at home also took place at this time, but unlike Goethe he did not show himself a natural actor, his sister reporting that he 'exaggerated everything through his lively enthusiasm'.[1]

Originally intended for the Church he was sent first to the local grammar-school and then, in obedience to the wish of Karl Eugen but against the inclination of his parents, to the Military Academy which the Duke had set up in his residence 'Solitude'. Here he was forced to study not theology but jurisprudence, being allowed, when the Academy transferred to Stuttgart in 1775, to change his course to medicine. The discipline was severe and deeply resented by the young poet. His thesis on *The Philosophy of Physiology* (1779) was rejected and the unwilling student forced to remain a further year 'in order that

---

[1] Quoted by Gustav Karpeles, *Schiller's Life*, in introduction to *Schillers Sämtliche Werke* (Max Hesses Verlag, Leipzig), pp. 7 and 9.

47

his fire might be somewhat damped down'.[2] A subsequent thesis *On the connection between the animal and spiritual natures in Man* (1780) was accepted, despite the inclusion of a quotation from his unfinished play *The Robbers* under the pretence that it was taken from an English tragedy. On leaving the Academy he began a short career as non-commissioned regimental physician in the Grenadiers.

In May 1781 he published *The Robbers* at his own expense, borrowing the money to do so. Two earlier plays, *The Student of Nassau* and *Cosmus von Medicis* have not survived.

The Robbers

Whatever its faults, the appeal of *The Robbers* as a youthful *cri du cœur* is irresistible. It lives today not only as one of the greatest *Sturm und Drang* plays, but a compellingly passionate revelation of the idealism and the impatience with corruption which are perennial to youth. Its central figures, conceived to show the evil influence of 'society' and the virtues of 'natural' man in Rousseauistic terms, attain a timeless significance.

Aspects of the plot recall the Gloucester story in *King Lear*. Count Maximilian von Moor has two sons, the first a natural rebel, the second an inveterate schemer. The younger son, Franz, persuades his father to disinherit his elder brother, revealing in his first soliloquy the heavy debt of Schiller's prose to Shakespeare's verse:

I have the greatest cause to be at odds with Nature and by my honour, I will make it felt. Why was I not the first to escape my mother's womb? Why not her only child? Why was I cursed so in my every feature? Why was I sundered out to look so ill? Even when I was born it seems they damned me. Why should I, of all men, wear a nose that fits the dwarfs of Lapland? The thick lips of a Moor? The eyes of some base Hottentot? By heaven it seems they piled the vilest traits of all mankind together and baked me from their sweepings. (Act I, Sc. I)

---

[2] Quoted by Gustav Karpeles, *Schiller's Life*, in introduction to *Schillers Sämtliche Werke* (Max Hesses Verlag, Leipzig), pp. 7 and 9.

When Karl, the elder son, learns that he is disinherited, he rejects the established social order with the same passion with which his creator had rebelled against the disciplines of the military academy, contrasting the vileness of man with the natural instincts of beasts, in a torrent of Rousseau-inspired anger:

Men!—Men! False hypocritical brood of crocodiles! Their eyes are water and their hearts brass! Kisses on their lips and swords within their bosoms! Lions and leopards feed their young, ravens sate their little ones on carnage—but Man! Man!—I have learned to suffer evil and can smile when angry foes presume to drink my health in blood from my own heart. But when blood-love itself becomes a traitor, when father-love is turned to a Megaera, why then take fire all human callousness! Change to a tiger, gentle-hearted lamb! And every fibre stretch itself to fury and destruction!

(Act I, Sc. II)

He becomes a robber-chieftain and, like Marlowe's Tamburlaine, rejoices in his own pitiless power. When one of the robbers is captured an entire town is sacked in the spectacular attempt to rescue him, a church is pillaged and the armaments store exploded 'over the heads of innocent Christians'. All this Karl boastingly admits to the Priest who upbraids him with his crimes, pointing as he does so to the rings he wears on his fingers:

I took this ruby from the finger of a minister whom I threw at the feet of his lord when he was hunting! Flattery had raised him from the dust to the height of first court-favourite. His neighbour's fall the foot-stool he had used to climb to his high rank! The tears of orphans floated him to triumph! I took this diamond from a Minister for Finance who sold position and office to the men who offered him most money, while he thrust wretched patriots from his door. I wear this agate in honour of a priest—one of your own gang—whom I throttled with my own hands as he wept in the open chancel for the decay of the Holy Inquisition! (Act II, Sc. III)

Meanwhile the plot advances at a pace in keeping with the

hectic rhetoric of the language. Franz tells his father that Karl has died, substantiating his lie by producing a sword whose bloody inscription indicates Karl's last wish that Franz should marry his brother's former beloved, Amalia. Amalia, faithful to her memories of Karl, rejects Franz. Count Moor faints at the news of his son's death and Franz, announcing that his father has died of shock, imprisons him in a lonely tower where only the kindness of one of Franz's servants enables him to survive. As a final touch of horror Franz buries a dead dog in the family vault in his father's stead.

The robbers are joined by Kosinsky, whose dramatic significance foreshadows later figures like the Black Knight in *The Maid of Orleans* and Johannes Parricida in *Tell*: he is a projection of thoughts in the protagonist's mind. Kosinsky joins the robbers because court intrigue has prevented his marrying the girl he loves: to underline the relationship between his circumstances and Karl's, Kosinsky's beloved is also called Amalia. The purpose of the Karl–Kosinsky scene, therefore, is to show how memories of former happiness persuade Karl to return home again. Its effect is to introduce the reunion of Karl and Amalia in a stylised manner, thereby subtly preventing the audience from feeling the realistic emotions of love and tenderness in such a degree as might conflict with the mood of the play as a whole. Up to now we have felt no pity for Karl's victims: they are shown as villainously corrupt and the plot has developed so quickly that we have had no time to consider it in realistic terms. Had Schiller allowed realism to invade the Amalia–Karl scenes of the second half of the play, the character of Karl would have presented the same conflict of romance and reality which we feel in Götz. But Karl is never allowed to become human in this way—he remains to the end the hero of a dream world whose crimes merely represent his rebellious courage and panache, and whose remorse betokens youthful idealism rather than mature soul-searching.

When Karl returns to his home neither Franz nor Amalia recognise him, though she is strangely attracted to him. Karl now feels he is too deep in sin to merit her hand. Without revealing his identity, he confesses that he loves a girl called Amalia—the scene is written as a stylised choric comment:

Karl Moor: How wretched she is! She loves one who is lost. Her love will never . . . ever . . . be rewarded.
Amalia: No, she will find that reward in heaven. Do they not say there is a better world where the wretched find rejoicing and those who have loved will find one another again?
Karl Moor: A world where every veil is torn away and love is born again in all its terror—A world that is called Eternity!—How cruel the fates have been to my Amalia.
Amalia: Cruel . . . when they allow you to love?
Karl Moor: Cruel, because she loves me. What if I were a man with blood on his hands? What if for every kiss *your* lover gave you, he could count a murder as well? My poor Amalia! Fate was cruel to her. (Act IV, Sc. IV)

Schiller's innate sense of theatre is revealed in this scene, for only such a stylised approach could preserve the unity of the play. It enables him to establish the basic paradox of Karl's character, his mixture of noble aspiration and villainous ruthlessness, without making this paradox unacceptable. Karl is a force like Marlowe's Tamburlaine, a poetic essence possessed of dynamic energy that unleashes itself on the stage. The strength of Schiller's creation, from the dramatic point of view, is that it *is* a paradox and hence acquires the first essential of a dramatic character, that of having more than one facet. Karl's reactions in the play are not realistically human, but they suggest humanity and hence engage our interest.

The same success in preserving the style of the play is evinced by the eventual repentance of the villainous Franz. In a scene with Pastor Moser (who shares his name with Schiller's teacher at the grammar-school) Franz discusses the possible existence of God. Here too reality might have intruded on the frenzied nightmare vision of the whole. But again realism is instinctively avoided—Franz's repentance is tinged with Marlovian defiance of heaven:

But I have no desire to be immortal. Whoever lives in heaven. . . .
I will compel Him to destroy me, provoke Him to such anger that
His own anger shall annihilate me. Tell me the greatest sin—the sin
that rouses up His fiercest wrath.   (Act V, Sc. I)

Driven mad and imagining the furies of hell upon him, Franz
takes his own life.

The conclusion of the play avoids all suggestion of a happy
ending—the vision of nobility co-existent with evil is followed
through with the kind of illogical logic that is in its very nature.
Karl rescues his father from imprisonment and Amalia recognises her lover at last. Yet Karl points out to her that marriage
is impossible, her nuptial torch could only be 'the flames that
lick round the cradles of babes and sucklings'. In despair the
poor girl threatens to kill herself and Karl's final gesture in
crime symbolises the essential super-human and elemental
contradiction in his being:

Amalia: No friend? Even amongst all these, no friend at all? . . .
    Why, then, Queen Dido teach me how to die! (*Is about to leave,
    a robber takes aim.*)
Robber Moor: Stop! . . . —Moor's bride shall only die by Moor's
    own hand. (*He murders her.*)   (Act V, Sc. II)

It is significant, if we bear Schiller's later plays in mind, that
having committed this final outrage, Karl does not immediately
kill himself. Had he done so, we might not have felt the
eventual triumph of the other side of his nature—his potential
sublimity—so strongly. Schiller stresses that it is not merely
the horror of a single moment in time which leads Karl to his
end, but the ability to respond to idealism which is part and
parcel of his conflicting nature. 'Can mortal sin then wipe out
mortal sin?', he asks. Can self-murder wipe out the murder of
others? Only, one feels, if it is demonstrably an act of genuine
repentance which, as far as tragic theatre is concerned, must be
clearly shown to be such. Schiller arranges such an unequivocal
act. Karl becomes a willing sacrifice, whose death will bring
advantage to another:

I remember I spoke to a poor wretch on my way, who works for a daily wage and has eleven children's mouths to feed. They will give a thousand Louis d'or to the man who delivers the great robber alive. I can do something to help the poor wretch.   (*Ibid.*)

When the play was first produced at Mannheim in 1782, Dalberg, the director of the theatre insisted on a playbill which somewhat obscured the magnificence of Schiller's vision, reducing it to terms of conventional eighteenth-century morality. Thus the bill insisted that the play showed 'the portrait of a lost but mighty soul' brought by excess of fire and evil company to descend to the 'depths of infamy and despair. As though anticipating the slogans of Hollywood in our time, it went on: 'Such a man as Robber Moor is one to weep for and hate, to detest and love.' Having pointed out that even in Franz Moor 'the inner worm of conscience is not killed', it concluded that the spectator would leave the theatre with the thought that 'the unseen hand of prescience also employs the evil-doer as the instrument of her intention and justice, and can untie the most intricate knotting of fate in the most surprising manner'.

Such a view of the play is unreal, because Schiller is not here concerned with morality but with poetry and romance. We do not weep for Karl Moor, neither do we hate him. We respond only to the magnificent, if youthful, idea which he embodies. It was only by an appeal to morality, however, that Dalberg felt he dared stage the play. Accordingly he cut the more extravagant passages and, for fear of giving offence, removed Pastor Moser from the text and turned the priest into a *Komissar*. Also afraid of the political implications of the piece, he refused to perform it in the contemporary costume which Schiller had intended. Schiller's objection, that the language of the play was essentially modern and would therefore sound out of place in period costume, went unheeded.

The first performance, according to contemporary report, 'turned the theatre into a madhouse'. Ladies in the audience were near to fainting, while gentlemen stamped their feet,   53 clenched their fists and created havoc in the auditorium. It was an instant success with the younger generation, but Duke Karl Eugen disapproved. Schiller—still a regimental physician—attended both the first and a subsequent performance without leave. He was punished by two weeks' confinement to barracks and instructed to write no more such seditious literature. The opinions of Rousseau were unwelcome to the founder of the Military Academy at Solitude. In September 1782 the poet fled to Mannheim under an assumed name, and thence to Bauerbach near Meiningen. A year passed before Dalberg judged it safe to stage any more of his plays, but when it seemed unlikely that the Duke would pursue him further, Schiller was given the post of resident dramatist at Mannheim, with the duty of providing three plays within the next twelve months. His salary was 300 Gulden a year, together with the entire proceeds of one performance of each play produced.

The Conspiracy of Fiesco at Genoa

The first play to be produced by Dalberg under the conditions of Schiller's new appointment was *Fiesco* 'a republican tragedy' the scene of which is laid in Genoa in 1547, where a group of conspirators, fearful of the tyranny of the Doge's nephew and prospective successor, Gianettino Doria, plan to declare a republic. Fiesco, Count of Lavagna, is described in the *dramatis personae* as: 'Head of the conspiracy. A young, slim, handsome man in the bloom of youth—Twenty-three years old—proud yet gracious—friendly yet possessed of majesty—courteously malleable yet cunning.' He is immediately recognisable, therefore, as a more complex figure than Karl Moor. In him the charm of a young rebel is united with the machinations of the courtier and the portrait of a villain-hero is attempted in more realistic style.

At the start of the play, Fiesco attempts to draw suspicion away from his plotting by adopting a deliberately frivolous attitude: though married to the virtuous Leonora, he is

2

3

4

5

6

7

Bei Orth hab ich durchreist Zu Wien will ich verbleiben
Ich bitt, mein Herr last mich in eure Bande schreiben

8

9

IO

conducting an affair with Gianettino's sister, Julia. An important clue to Schiller's development of this part of the plot is found in his thesis *On the connection between the animal and spiritual natures in man*, where he says:

Catiline was a libertine before he became a murderer and Doria [*i.e.* Gianettino Doria] deceived himself greatly in believing that he had nothing to fear from the libertine, Fiesco.

Though Fiesco's real intentions are left insufficiently clear to the audience in the early stages, and he is, therefore, in danger of forfeiting their sympathy, his amatory intrigue leads to the dramatically effective scene in which Leonora is made to overhear his spurning of his mistress. As the proud coquette, Julia, is forced to her knees before him, he draws back the curtain to reveal Leonora with the words:

Here is my wife! A goddess among women! (*Leonora embraces him.*)
(Act IV, Sc. XII)

If Fiesco's libertinism is shown as merely a means to the fulfilment of his revolutionary ideals, however, his other fault, that of personal ambition, remains unexcused. Again Schiller has chosen a hero whose nature contains irreconcilable opposites. Starting as a revolutionary idealist, Fiesco ends by desiring power for himself. Leonora tries in vain, using Rousseauistic arguments, to awaken him to his danger:

In the stormy regions of the throne, the tender plant of love is doomed to perish. A man's heart—even if that man be Fiesco himself—is not large enough for two all-powerful gods. Gods who have such spite! Love may shed tears and can understand tears: the lust for power has only brazen eyes where pearls of tenderness may never form. (Act IV, Sc. XIV)

She begs Fiesco to flee with her: 'Let us throw all this glittering nothingness in the dust, let us live only in the romantic regions of love. . . . Our life will rise to the Creator like the pure flute-like melody of spring-water.' No sooner has she said these

55

E

words than cannon-fire is heard off stage—an indication that the revolution has begun. Leonora, dressed in man's clothes, fights for her husband's cause. Gianettino is killed by one of the conspirators and finding his scarlet cloak and hat she dresses herself in them, only to be mistaken in her disguise for Gianettino himself, and slain by her own husband.

Fiesco thus resembles Karl Moor in killing the woman he loves. Once again it was Schiller's intention to demonstrate this villainy as arising from the mixture of sublimity and evil in his hero's soul. Yet the circumstances of the plot scarcely depict this adequately, for Leonora's death is brought about by mere accident of mistaken identity, not, except indirectly, by Fiesco's lust for power. In the first case there is no real motive for Leonora's adopting her disguise. She does so as the result of a whim:

My hero shall embrace a heroine! My Brutus hold a Roman in his arms! (Act V, Sc. V)

In the second case, Fiesco's motive for killing her is only that of hatred for the supposed Gianettino, the more complex motive of his personal ambition is left out of account in the brief but important Act V, Sc. XI (here given *in toto*):

Fiesco. Leonora appears at the back in Gianettino's scarlet cloak.
Fiesco (*noticing her, steps forward then retreats, muttering fiercely*): That plume and cloak! I know them! (*Comes nearer, powerfully.*) I know them well. (*Furiously as he rushes at her and strikes her down.*) If you have three lives, rise again and walk! (*Leonora falls with a broken cry. A victory march is heard: drums, horns and oboes.*)

While the irony of the victory march, sounding at the moment of Fiesco's greatest misfortune, is splendid theatre, one cannot help feeling that the dramatist in Schiller has outstripped the poet at this point. The outward events are exciting but they fail to illuminate the inner vision of the play.

The weakness of this scene is the more remarkable if we compare Leonora's death with Fiesco's own. Here Schiller was compelled to depart from the facts of history and gave his reasons for doing so in the Preface:

The true catastrophe of the conspiracy, whereby Count Fiesco perished as the result of an unhappy accident when his desire was near fulfilment, had to be completely changed, for the nature of drama will not tolerate the finger of chance or the direct interference of Providence.

Fiesco's death is, therefore, carefully designed to avoid the 'interference of Providence' which is so apparent in Leonora's. Gianettino having been killed, Fiesco becomes Duke of Genoa and in the final scene encounters Verrina, a fellow-conspirator of staunch republican principles who joined the plot to avenge the rape of his daughter by Gianettino. Throughout the play Verrina has been aware of the personal ambition of Fiesco. Seeing the new Duke in all his finery, he urges him to 'Cast away the purple!', the symbol of majesty first introduced to hide the bloodshed of tyrants. When Fiesco insists that his nature is unchanged by his new office, Verrina persuades him to free the galley-slaves as the first sign of his clemency. In a last attempt to stem the Count's ambition, Verrina, whose proud principles have hitherto refused to kneel to mortal man, falls down before him and repeats his plea:

Verrina: . . . Throw aside the purple!
Fiesco: Get up! And anger me no more.
Verrina (*with decision*): I will get up—and anger you no more. (*They are standing on the gang-plank that leads to one of the galleys.*) The Duke has precedence. (Act V, Sc. XVI)

As Fiesco goes up the plank, Verrina seizes his cloak from behind and hurls him into the sea below. Here, one feels, poet and dramatist are working to the same end. Indeed, the poet need say very little: the earlier scenes have made the conflict between Verrina and Fiesco so clear that the final action is its own comment—the dramatist does the poet's work for him.

On various other occasions in the play visual effect corresponds exactly with the poet's intention. Thus, the *dramatis*

57

personae gives careful indication of the colours to be worn: Andreas Doria, the Doge of Genoa, and his son Gianettino are dressed in scarlet, symbolic of their office; Leonora, Julia and all the nobles wear black. The use of masques and disguises, together with the device of bringing the conspirators together at a theatrical entertainment, portrays the deception and intrigue of the piece in visual terms.[3] Stage directions at the beginning of acts indicate the appropriate atmosphere:

Act I : *A hall in Fiesco's palace. In the distance we hear dance-music and the tumult of a ball.*

Act III: *An eery wilderness. Verrina and Bourgognino come through the night.*

Act V: *After midnight. A broad street in Genoa.—Here and there lamps are burning in some of the houses. Gradually they go out. At the back of the stage we see the Thomas Gate, which is still closed. In perspective distance the sea. A few people cross the street with hand lanterns. They are followed by the Watch and the Patrol. Everything is quiet. Only the waves of the sea are somewhat restless.*

Despite the use of spectacle, the excitement and universal interest of the theme and the introduction of refreshing humour in the character of the rascally Moor who serves Fiesco, the play was not successful when first produced and has never become one of Schiller's most popular pieces. The main reason for this, perhaps, is that he relied too greatly on the sheer physical attractiveness of his hero (noted, as we have seen, in the *dramatis personae*) to gain our initial sympathy. We are left too long in the dark about Fiesco's real motives. The intrigue which surrounds him robs him of the 'natural' sublimity of Karl Moor and hence, though he gains our interest, we never quite feel the pity and fear which tragedy requires.

Intrigue and Love

Schiller's next play returns to the Germany of his own time. In

---

[3] See H. B. Garland, *Schiller the Dramatic Writer* (Oxford, 1969), Chapter II, for further discussion of this point.

a small Court, Major Ferdinand von Walter, son of the President, falls in love with Luise Miller, daughter of a musician. Marriage between them is, therefore, socially unacceptable. The girl's parents are arrested and in order to secure their freedom she is forced by the President's secretary to write a love letter to the Court Chamberlain—a man for whom she has no affection. The letter is shown to Ferdinand and arouses his jealously. Since Luise has been sworn to silence as a condition of her parents' freedom, she dares not reveal to him the plot that has been laid against her. Supposing her unfaithful, Ferdinand poisons Luise and, on learning the truth from her dying lips, takes his own life.

In choice of the theme of class conflict, *Intrigue and Love* looks back to Lessing's *Emilia Galotti* and also anticipates much nineteenth- and twentieth-century drama. It is noteworthy for its use of realism in many scenes and the fact that Schiller denotes characterisation by means of contrasting styles of speech. Thus, in the opening scene, Luise's father is characterised by his bourgeois bluntness, her mother by a tendency to malapropisms and importations from the French:[4]

Frau Miller: Hold your horses a moment, do! You blaze up on the least provocation! All I'm saying is that we mustn't *dischguster* the Herr Major because he's the President's son.
Miller: And that's the fly in the ointment! That's exactly why the whole thing has got to be over and done with today! If he's a decent father, the President ought to thank me for it. —You take a brush to my red velvet coat and I'll see about an audience with His Excellency. I shall tell His Excellency 'Your son has cast his eye on my daughter. My daughter is too lowly-born to be that gentleman's wife—and too precious by far to be his whore! And there's an end to the matter! —I'm not called Miller for nothing.   (Act I, Sc. I)

In the same way the character of the President is brought out in

---

[4] See Garland, *op. cit.*, chapter III, for further analysis of speech styles in the play.

Act I, Sc. VII by an impatient sarcasm which manifests itself in broken sentences:

Masterly! Faultless! Magnificent! After thirty years we're back to lecture one! Such a pity my fifty-year-old head has grown too tough for learning. But—for fear we let this unusual talent rust—I'll give you a companion with whom you can indulge your motley madness. —You will make up your mind—make up your mind today—to take a wife.

In the scene in which Luise is forced by Wurm, the aptly named secretary to the President, to write the fatal letter, the naturalism of the staccato dialogue surprises us with its modernity:

Wurm: There's only one way.
Luise: Only this way?
Wurm: Even your father wants. . . .
Luise: Even my father? What way is it, then?
Wurm: Quite easy for you.
Luise: Nothing is more difficult to bear than shame.
Wurm: If you only agree to give up the Major—set him free. . . .
Luise: From the love he bears me?—Why do you torment me? Why offer me a choice when I'm compelled?
Wurm: My dear young lady, that was not my meaning. The Major will renounce *you*—of his own accord.
Luise: He will not do that!
Wurm: So it, indeed, appears. Would we have turned to you, if you weren't the only person who could help us?
Luise: How can I make him hate me?
Wurm: We must see! Sit down.
Luise (*confused*): In heaven's name man! What are you trying to do?
Wurm: Sit down! Write! There's the pen—paper and ink.
Luise (*sits, in great distress*): What am I to write? Who am I to write to?
Wurm: Your father's hangman.
Luise: O, how you can screw souls to the rack! (*Takes a pen.*)
Wurm (*dictating*): 'Dear Sir'—
Luise (*writes with a trembling hand.*)

Wurm: 'Already three unbearable days have passed—have passed—
and we have not seen each other.'
Luise *(stops short and lays down the pen)*: Who is this letter to?
Wurm: Your father's hangman!
Luise: O, dear God! (Act III, Sc. VI)

This realism is mixed, however, with the more flamboyant style found in Schiller's earlier plays. Initially the contrast between the two works well. It is acceptable that Ferdinand, the young aristocrat with sensitive feelings and good education, should express himself more eloquently than the Millers. If his language is not realistic it is at least excused by the conventions of drama, and the character gains our sympathy by the spirit with which he rejects his father's proposal of a diplomatic career with all its attendant duplicity:

My ideas of greatness and good-fortune are not entirely yours! Your pleasure seldom manifests itself except through corruption. Envy, fear, damnation—those are the wretched mirrors that reflect the smile of princely rulers. Tears, despair and curses are the nauseous food such happy potentates glut themselves upon, before they rise up drunk and reel before the eternal throne of God! But my ideal of happiness contains itself more closely in my soul. All my desires lie buried in my heart. (Act I, Sc. VII)

The contrast between Ferdinand's frankness and his father's cunning provides the scene with a complexity of minor crises and climaxes which build to an exciting close. The father, suspicious of Ferdinand's love for Luise, proposes that he should marry Lady Milford, an Englishwoman who is the Prince's mistress. Ferdinand rejects her as a notorious whore. The President appears to give ground, agreeing with his son's estimate of Milford and instantly suggesting another choice, a lady of irreproachable reputation. Ferdinand is trapped. His only answer is that he cannot love the lady in question and hence the old man's suspicions of a liaison with Luise are confirmed. After all, he declares, his son shall marry Lady Milford, and the scene ends with a bravura passage that shows

61

how well Schiller had learned to write for a stage dominated by operatic conventions, at the same time using those conventions for something as alien to them as social criticism:

President: . . . Go at once! The parade's already started. As soon as you're dismissed, go to the Lady.—When I come on the scene whole Dukedoms tremble! Let's see if one hot-headed boy can get the better of me! (*Goes out and returns.*) I tell you, boy, you'll be there—or else you'll answer for it. (*Exit.*)

Ferdinand (*recovering from his stunned condition*): Gone? Were those a *father's* words?—Yes, I will go to her!—I'll go to her—and say such things to her—hold up a mirror! O contemptible whore!— And if you still demand my hand—then in the presence of the assembled court, the army and the people—Put on the armour of your English pride!—I will spurn you! I, a German youth!
(*Ibid.*)

Unfortunately Schiller does not keep this style only for Ferdinand and the members of the Court circle—it is also extended to Luise in certain scenes and hence she fails to become a totally convincing character. This is particularly true of Act IV, Sc. VII where she confronts her powerful rival, Lady Milford, using images and arguments that scarcely suggest a humble musician's daughter of sixteen:

O dear God! Grant me that blindness which alone can reconcile me to my barbaric fate!—An insect in a drop of water feels content, as though it were in heaven—so happy, so content till it is told of oceans where the mighty fleets go sailing and the great whales play.

This kind of speech seems to be suggested not by the character of the speaker, but rather by the subject matter of the scene. Luise is about to renounce her claims on Ferdinand and threatens to kills herself. Doubtless the situation could have been handled in terms of the realism of the earlier scenes, but Schiller was attracted here, as always, to the idealism of self-sacrifice. It is worth noting that this theme comes into his plays long before his intensive study of Kant—it is present at the end of *The Robbers* when Karl Moor delivers himself up to the poor man with eleven starving children. In this play it is present not only with Luise in Act IV, Sc. VII, but in the monologue of Lady Milford which follows in Sc. VIII.

I, too, have power to give up things I love! . . . Creep into hiding weak and suffering woman! Sweet golden images of love, sail on! . . . Virtue, I throw myself into your arms! Receive a penitent daughter, your Emilia!—How light my heart is suddenly! How happy I feel! How elated! Majestic as the sinking sun, today I will forsake my pinnacle of greatness and leave my heart alone to bear me company in this proud banishment. . . . It must be done at once —before the charms of him I love renew the beating conflict of my heart.

Thus the stress of these two scenes is on idealism, though an attempt is made to keep contact with realism at the same time. In Lady Milford's 'How light my heart is suddenly! How happy I feel! How elated!' we have already something of the sense of moral freedom to be found in later figures like Mary Stuart and St. Joan. But Milford is far from declaring 'The pain is short. The joy will last forever'. She still fears that the sight of Ferdinand may weaken her resolve and her sensuous instincts thus betray her spirit. This, it may be argued, is true to human nature. Indeed it is, but it has the effect of underlining the melodramatic nature of both Milford's and Luise's gestures. The same is true at the end of the play, where realism and idealism again co-exist and conflict. Ferdinand gives poison to Luise in a glass of lemonade. As a piece of realism this is unexceptionable—a girl of Luise's class would perhaps have drunk no wine—yet how prosaic it seems compared with the wine that poisons Gertrude in *Hamlet*, the fire which Portia swallows in *Julius Caesar* and the asp that Cleopatra lays to her breast! These Shakespearean characters die 'by strange manner',—a manner far stranger than that which kills Luise Miller —yet in the theatre they have a sublimity lacking in her death. The division between melodrama and tragedy depends ultimately not so much on the events presented but the way in

63

which they are presented. *Intrigue and Love* begins as a pseudo-realistic drama and as such is tightly wrought and full of theatrical life. Yet it does not touch the heights of Schiller's greatest plays and by its very employment of realistic convention remains almost unique amongst his works. Thereafter all his dramas are in verse, a medium which enabled him to combine his theatrical flair and idealistic tendencies more successfully and to achieve his status as one of the great dramatists of the world.

CHAPTER FOUR

The Amateur Theatre at Weimar

Intrigue and Love was written in 1783, *Stella* in 1775. After writing these plays each poet turned away from *Sturm und Drang* theatre and began to move towards what has come to be known as 'Weimar Classicism'. The foundations of this new style were already laid before Schiller arrived in Weimar in 1787 and the task of the present chapter, therefore, is to outline how this occurred. Three main headings will be considered: (1) The influence of the Court of Weimar on Goethe, (2) The plays of Goethe that were performed by the Amateur Theatre there and (3) The techniques of the Amateur Theatre.

The Influence of the Court of Weimar on Goethe

Of the many independent States which made up Germany in the eighteenth century, the Dukedom of Saxe-Weimar (now included in the German Democratic Republic) was amongst the smallest and poorest. Once the scene of Luther's famous attack on Tetzel's indulgences, it retained a strong Protestant tradition but no longer played a significant part in either the religious or political affairs of Europe. Largely an agricultural region, its Court was noted for its love of music (the young Johann Sebastian Bach, born at Eisenach, was Court Organist and Concert Master 1708–16) and its liberal culture. From 1758–75 it was ruled by the Duchess Anna Amalia, niece of

Frederick the Great, who did not follow her uncle's example of imitating French art, but encouraged native German talent and ideas. Her son, Karl August, whose education she had supervised, first met Goethe in Frankfurt in 1774, having previously read, and been delighted by *Götz von Berlichingen*, a play whose wild enthusiasms appealed to his own youthful and over-exuberant spirits. A year later, on attaining his majority and becoming the ruler of Weimar, Karl August invited the poet to visit the Duchy.

Goethe, by this time famous as the author both of *Götz* and the sentimental novel *Werther*, lived up to the extravagances of both during the first few weeks in his new surroundings, the Duke becoming the eager companion of his escapades. After two months of frivolity, however, Goethe decided to return home and was only persuaded to stay by the Duke's offering him a seat on the Council. Since neither his wild behaviour nor his father's bourgeois status seemed to warrant such a position, eyebrows were raised in certain quarters. But the poet took his new tasks extremely seriously and as he reformed his own ways was always conscious of his duty to lead Karl August (whom he was allowed to address by the intimate *Du*) along similar paths. In 1779 Goethe was made Privy Councillor. In 1782 he became Minister of Finance and was granted the rank of nobility (hence his subsequent right to style himself *von* Goethe).

Goethe's official duties in Weimar were numerous and exacting. He occupied himself with the mines at Ilmenau and eventually succeeded in reopening them, he managed the finances of the Duchy, acted as Commissioner for Roads, organised a Fire Brigade, undertook the direction of the War Department and reconstructed the armed forces, and went on endless tours of the Duke's territory in an untiring attempt to improve the lot of the ninety thousand or so inhabitants. He was also responsible for the direction of the Court Amateur Theatre (1775–83) and the professional Court Theatre (1791–1817). Though Weimar was small—the town itself numbering at that time only about six thousand inhabitants—these many duties gave Goethe a sense of responsibility and seriousness which are reflected in all his subsequent literary works. The ideal of 'Humanity' which was expressed at the end of *Stella* became deepened by experience, while at the same time Goethe was exploring an astonishingly wide intellectual field. Conversant with the literatures of Greece and Rome, modern Italy, France and England, he was also a keen amateur artist and a scientist of distinction in his own day. His theory of light and colour, in which he opposes the principles of Newton, is now, perhaps, only of historical interest, but his works on the metamorphosis of plants and animal morphology anticipate the work of Darwin. With all this went literary activity which embraced lyric poetry, epic, satire, novels, criticism, autobiography and drama.

A considerable steadying influence on Goethe during his first ten years at Weimar was Frau Charlotte von Stein, the wife of the Ducal Master of Horse, for whom he formed a passionate spiritual attachment. His letters to her (published in three volumes between 1848–51) form one of the most important sources for studying the development of his personality at this time, and her influence is also to be found in his drama. After Goethe left for Italy in 1786 his passion cooled and their friendship was broken off after he set up house with Christiane Vulpius (mother of his son August) in 1788. From 1788–1805 he met Frau von Stein seldom, but thereafter the friendship was resumed on a less passionate basis until her death in 1827.

Weimar already had a tradition of encouraging the arts. As we have seen, opera was performed there in the late seventeenth century and when Duke Ernst Augustus Constantin (father of Karl August) became ruler in 1756 an official company of Court Actors was formed. This, however, was disbanded after his death in 1758, when his widow, Anna Amalia, was forced for financial reasons to restrict social activities. She continued none the less to patronise music and painting. In 1768 a new company of Court Actors was formed by Koch, the former associate of Gottsched and Caroline Neuber. Koch's taste was particularly for *Singspiele* (plays with music) and as a result Weimar has sometimes been called 'the cradle of German operetta'. When Koch left in 1771 to go to Berlin, this musical tradition was continued by the Seyler–Ekhof company, who also presented a wide repertoire of 'straight' plays (including Lessing, Molière, Marivaux, Goldoni and Cumberland amongst others). Performances were given three times a week before an invited audience which was by no means confined to the immediate Court circle. All expenses for costumes and scenery were met by Anna Amalia, even food and wine being included 'when it pleases a poet to have them served in a play'.[1] With Ekhof as leading actor and director, the Duchy possessed a theatre which fulfilled the functions of a National Theatre though still nominally a private one. It lasted, however, only until 1774 when the theatre was destroyed by fire. Ekhof moved to Gotha and Weimar was forced to satisfy its taste for theatricals by amateur performances in various adapted buildings. Such performances had started even before Goethe's arrival, being partially inspired, perhaps, by the amateur productions that took place in other Courts at the time.

The Plays of Goethe performed by the Amateur Theatre

Many of the plays by Goethe performed by the Amateur Theatre were short, some like *The Fair at Plundersweilen* (1778) amounting to little more than satirical charades. Only the prose version of *Iphigenia in Tauris*, which will be considered at the end of this section, can be classed as a major work, though there is much of both stylistic and biographical interest in the other plays.

Pieces such as *Erwin and Elmira* (1776) and *Jery and Bätely* (1779) are delightful examples of the *Singspiel* genre and the

---

[1] Quoted by Ernst Pasqué, *Goethe's Theaterleitung in Weimar* (Leipzig, 1863), vol. I, p. 23.

first, which had been written in Frankfurt at the time of
Goethe's affair with Lili Schönemann, is a short pastoral play
on the jealousy of young love, containing a ballad that is a
companion piece to *The Hedge-Rose* (*Heidenröslein*):

Rosa: A violet grew upon the mead
             Whose modesty no eye would heed,
             The sweetest, tenderest flower.
Valerio: A shepherdess then came that way
             Whose step was light, whose heart was gay.
             Along, along,
             Along she came and sang.
Elmira: The violet sighed 'That I might be
             The sweetest bloom in Arcady
             One passing quarter-hour,
             Till plucked and by her hand caressed
             And softly gathered to her breast!
             A while, a while,
             In heaven there to hang!'
Rosa: Alas, alas, the maid passed by,
             The violet failed to catch her eye.
             She trampled on the flower.
Valerio: It wilted, died rejoicing still:
             'If die I must, then die I will
             By you, by you.
             I die by your sweet will.'
All Three: 'If die I must, then die I will
             By you, by you.
             I die by your sweet will.'

Such works not only remind us of Goethe's power as a lyric poet,
but also anticipate the use of lyrical and allegorical drama which
he was later to employ in *Faust II*. Whereas, however, whole
passages of the second part of Goethe's *Faust* seem to defy
conventional staging, in plays such as *Erwin and Elmira, Jery
and Bätely, The Fisher Girl* (1782) and *Claudine von Villa-Bella*
(1776) we find swift-moving plots and plenty of action.

    Jery and Bätely, inspired by a journey to Switzerland with
Karl August, is a lively bucolic farce in which Bätely disdains   69

her lover, Jery, till his soldier friend, Thomas, decides to teach her a lesson. He frightens her by driving cattle on to her land and smashing the windows of her house—intending to allow Jery to come to rescue her. Jery, however, takes Thomas's efforts seriously and hence a real fight takes place between them in which Jery has to be defeated. But Bätely's heart is touched by his efforts to protect her and all ends happily.

In *The Fisher Girl* (1782) a similar piece of country intrigue (the decision of Dortchen, the fisher-girl to pretend to have drowned herself in order to make her father and lover more appreciative of her when she is returned to them) provides even greater opportunity for action. This play was staged in the open air at Tiefurt and reached its spectacular climax in the scene in which the villagers search for the missing girl. Goethe's own note on the scene is as follows:

The impact of the entire play was calculated on this scene. The spectators sat, without realising it, in such a manner that they had the entire river winding down in front of them. At this moment in the action torches were first seen moving in the immediate distance. As more cries went up they appeared in the far distance as well. Then flickering fires flamed forth on the tongues of land that jutted into the water. The light of these fires and their reflection revealed the objects nearest to them very clearly, while the surrounding region still lay in the depths of night. Seldom can a more beautiful effect have been witnessed. It lasted, with a number of variations, to the end of the play when the entire tableau blazed once more into full light.

Such adventurous staging illustrates the practical nature of Goethe's work with the Amateur Theatre. It was here that he learned much of his craft as a playwright, becoming increasingly aware that the work of a stage poet must allow for, and is enhanced by, the contributions of actor, director and scenic designer. Thus *Claudine von Villa-Bella*—an operetta that is full of processions, disguises, violent action, changing scenes and which even includes a breeches-part—contains the following stage direction, indicative of the debt the poet owes to the actor:

The entire development which the poetry can only briefly indicate and the music expresses more fully, will only come alive through the actions of the actors. Alonzo's astonishment and how he gradually takes hold of himself having had the circumstances explained to him, passing from astonishment to astonishment and finally to calm understanding; the tenderness of Pedro and Claudine; the more vigorous passion of Carlos and Lucinda ... all this the actors are to express in a lively, appropriate and harmonious manner and enliven the music and dialogue with a pre-rehearsed pantomime.

And in *Lila* we find a direction which indicates that the whole provision of ballet in the fourth act is left completely to the taste of the dancing-master. At the same time the stress on 'harmonious' (*übereinstimmend*) action in *Claudine von Villa Bella* is significant, for this sense that all aspects of theatre must be directed towards a common end, the expression of beauty on the stage, was to be characteristic of Weimar Classicism.

Some of the plays of this early period clearly mark individual stages of Goethe's progress towards the ideal of harmony. The short play *Brother and Sister* (1776) presents a hero, Wilhelm (played by Goethe himself on the Weimar stage), who is reformed by his love for a certain Charlotte (in whom we may recognise Charlotte von Stein). The Charlotte of the play has died before the action begins and Wilhelm speaks of her in the following terms:

She was too good for this earth! How often have I told you—that I became a different person through knowing her. I can't tell you how I suffered when I came back and saw how I had wasted all my father left me. I dared not offer her my hand in marriage, I could do nothing to make her state more bearable. For the first time in my life I felt compelled to earn my own living in a decent and proper way—to tear myself up from the listless, aimless existence that I'd lived through so miserably from one day to the next.

In Wilhelm's desire to forsake the aimlessness of his previous existence it is easy to recognise the new Goethe. Indeed the

71

F

restraint and idealism promoted by Frau von Stein pervade the play. On her death Charlotte entrusts her daughter, Marianne, to Wilhelm's keeping and he brings her up as his sister. Only when a neighbour, Fabrice, seeks her hand in marriage is the truth of her birth revealed. Yet already Marianne has decided that her love for her 'brother' is so deep that she can never leave him, and as the curtain falls the pair prepare to be married. Though the subject matter might seem to raise the possibility of incestuous guilt in the minds of the protagonists, it never does so. The play remains on the level of idealistic romance throughout and its unity of style reveals Goethe's growing maturity as a dramatist.

Another play indicative of his changing ideas is the 'dramatic caprice' *The Triumph of Sensibility* (1778) which satirises the cult of sensibility inspired by such works as *The Sorrows of the Young Werther*. Prince Oronaro is a man 'of such delicate and extremely sensitive nerves that he must protect himself carefully from the air and the swift vicissitudes of the times of day'. Accordingly he carries round with him a 'travelling' nature which we see assembled on the stage. Merkulo, his gentleman, explains its wonders to Sora and Mana, two ladies-in-waiting:

Sora: Forgive me, but what is in that box there? May one know?
Merkulo: . . . Here we offer the most exquisite delights of the sensitive souls of our nation. In this box are bubbling streams.
Mana: O!
Merkulo: In this one is contained the song of birds! Loveliest, loveliest birdsong!
Mana: Well—why not, indeed?
Merkulo: And in this large box we packed the light of the moon.
Sora: It isn't possible! Do let us see it!
Merkulo: It is not in my power to do so. Only the Prince understands how to set these splendours in motion and bring them to life. He alone, and he only, may feel their joys. I can only let you see the raw materials.
Mana: Then we must beg the Prince to set his toy-machine going for us.

Merkulo: For heaven's sake! You must know nothing about it! The Prince wouldn't have the slightest idea what you were talking about if you referred to his amusements as *toys*! My dear young lady, we all of us take our amusements very seriously—usually far more seriously than we do our business. . . . I should be delighted to show you our curiosities . . . if only the decorations in this room were in any way commensurate with the Nature that's imprisoned in these chests.

Mana: You can't ask illusion to be as perfect as that!

Sora: We can soon do something about it. After all we have the tapestries—and they show nothing but woods and prospects.

Merkulo: Most charming!

Sora: Hey! (*A servant enters.*) Tell the Court upholsterer to let down the tapestries at once.

Merkulo: And I shan't fail you either.

(*Music.*)

(*He gives a sign and at that moment, as the scene is changed into woodland, the boxes turn into grassy seats, rocks, bushes and so on. The box above the arbour turns into clouds. The designer will be careful to see that the whole is harmonious and attractive, making a strongly felt contrast with the scenery that disappears.*)

Merkulo: Bravo! Bravo!

Sora: O how beautiful!

(*They examine everything with the greatest curiosity as long as the music continues.*)

Mana: It's the loveliest scenery in the world!

Merkulo: Forgive me, *not* scenery! We call it artificial nature. For you will observe that the word 'Nature' must be present on all occasions. (Act II)

In the following act the various machines (some details of whose construction will be given later) are made to work at the Prince's command: *The waterfalls begin to rush, the birds to sing and the moon to shine.* The arbour opens and reveals a life-size doll from whose bosom are extracted various classics of 'Sensibility' including Rousseau's *Héloise* and the author's own *Werther.* Symbolically, they are 'mixed with chaff', for everything about

73

Oronaro is shown to be ridiculous—his travelling nature, his doll-mistress and his opinions. Yet the satire is essentially gentle, using a kind of Brechtian alienation technique in reverse. The 'travelling' scenery of Oronaro did not materially differ from the ordinary scenery of the Weimar stage. In drawing attention to its artificiality, Goethe at the same time exploits the magic of its illusion. The aim is not to 'alienate' us and induce critical reflection, but rather to use a more sophisticated form of fantasy to comment on a naïve one. In Coleridgean terms the world of Oronaro could be termed 'fancy', whereas the world of the play itself is 'imaginative': a disciplined artistic form is used to reveal the self-indulgence of private dreams.

A similar theme is found in *Lila* (1777). Just as in *The Triumph of Sensibility* the Prince accepts scenery for nature, so in this play Baroness Lila mistakes disguised human beings for supernatural creatures. Believing her husband to have been killed, she falls into a distraction in which she imagines him beset by evil spirits. The only way to return her to her senses, the doctor declares, is to 'cure fantasy by fantasy'. The Court therefore diguise themselves as spirits and the operetta proceeds as though this illusion were in fact a reality, until Lila is cured and reunited with her husband. There is, however, a great difference between Lila and Oronaro, which the doctor points to when he says: 'She, herself, believes that she can gain back her husband by means of patience and resolution.' Lila has the self-discipline needed to turn private fantasy into poetic truth. The doctor goes on:

If only music and dancing can surround her and tear her from this dark grief into which she has fallen—if the unlooked for appearance of fantastic forms can only strengthen her in her hopes and imaginings—as most certainly it will—then we shall have achieved enough. (Act I)

Thus the doctrine of the purity of human instinct preached by Rousseau is not entirely rejected, but modified by insistence on the need for self-discipline. It is not merely fantasy which returns to Lila her husband, but also the power of her love for him:

> What love and fantasy destroy
> Fancy and love give back again.

The theme of the relationship between instinct and self-discipline is further explored in the most important of all the plays staged by the Weimar Amateur Theatre *Iphigenia in Tauris* (1779).

The Prose Version of Iphigenia in Tauris

There are two versions of *Iphigenia*: the prose version performed in 1779 and the verse one which has become the standard theatrical text today. The relationship between the two in respect of character and action is very close and for this reason discussion of these aspects will be left until later, when *Iphigenia* is examined alongside Goethe's other major plays of the 'classical' period. Here we shall take only two questions: the reflection of the poet's maturing ideas in the general scheme of the play, and the staging of the prose version.

Goethe's *Iphigenia in Tauris* differs from Euripides' chiefly in its conception of the heroine. All other differences ultimately spring from this. In Goethe's play, Iphigenia, daughter of Agamemnon, exerts an essentially humanising force on the kingdom of Tauris. Brought there as Diana's priestess after her father's attempt to sacrifice her at Aulis, she succeeds in abolishing the ancient bloody rite that decreed all strangers to the country should be slain as offerings to the Goddess. She is also convinced that in her alone lies the hope of redemption for her accursed line. Only if she can retain her purity will the curse of the House of Tantalus be lifted. Therefore, when Thoas, King of Tauris, asks her hand in marriage she refuses him. His answer is to demand the renewal of the custom of sacrifice, revealing as he does so that: 'Two strangers whom we found hidden in the caves beside the sea, and who bode evil to my land, have been captured.' The strangers are Iphigenia's brother, Orestes, and his friend, Pylades. They have been sent to Tauris at Apollo's command and believe their mission to be, what in fact it *is* in the play of Euripides, to return the image of Apollo's sister, Diana, from Tauris to Delphi. In fact, however, they have mistaken the intent of the oracle, for it speaks in Goethe's play only of the return of the 'sister' from the shore of Tauris. Thus, at the end of the play, Orestes is able to reinterpret its meaning: the God had not intended the reuniting of his sister's image with his own on the altar of Delphi, but the reunion of the human brother and sister, Iphigenia and Orestes. The will of the Gods is therefore coincident with the highest desires of man and as Iphigenia says of the Gods to Thoas:

> They only speak to us through our heart.

Thus an essentially eighteenth-century gloss is given to the ancient myth. Natural human instinct, however, is not seen in the play as sufficient in itself to guide us to virtue. Whereas in Euripides, Iphigenia tricks Thoas and steals the image, in Goethe's play the immediate instinct to save her brother's life at all cost, is resisted. Conscious always of her mission 'to return home with pure hands and with pure heart and redeem our house', Iphigenia recognises that instinct must be tempered by idealism. Staking everything on absolute truthfulness, she reveals to Thoas that the stranger she is asked to sacrifice is her brother. She, thus, relies on the 'humanity' of the barbarian King, who in the past has shown her such kindness, to grant their freedom. Even when Thoas challenges Orestes to single combat, she pleads against bloodshed and discord and finally her pleas are heard. Orestes, Pylades and Iphigenia return to Greece and Thoas is left alone.

The influence of Frau von Stein on the character of Iphigenia is frequently noted by critics and is undoubtedly present. At the same time, the notion of idealised womanhood as exerting refining and redemptive force on mankind cannot be attributed to her alone. It is a universal idea, present in many literatures and religions of the world, and is foreshadowed to some extent by the figure of Cäcilie in the first version of *Stella*. Whereas, however, Cäcilie's concept of 'Humanity' leads to the doubtful morality of a *ménage à trois*, Iphigenia's decision to appeal to Thoas bespeaks the greatest moral responsibility in all respects.

The play was first performed on 6 April 1779 and great care was taken to establish the appropriate classical atmosphere. The stage was covered with a green cloth to deaden the noise of the actors' feet and the proscenium arch was painted to represent marble pillars. At the back of the stage the temple of Diana was shown in the half-round, while four pairs of wings represented the grove. Goethe played the part of Orestes and the following description of his performance has been left to us by Christoph Hufeland, the son of the physician-in-ordinary to the Court:

Never shall I forget the impression which he made in Greek costume as Orestes. One believed one was watching Apollo. Never has such a union of physical and spiritual beauty been seen in a man. . . . I have never met with a man who was at one and the same time so richly endowed by heaven both physically and spiritually, and who could accordingly in very truth present the image of humanity at its most perfect.[2]

The Techniques of the Amateur Theatre

In the first production of *Iphigenia*, Pylades was played by Prince Constantin (Karl August's brother), Thoas by Knebel, the princes' tutor, and Arkas by Seidler, another court tutor. When the play was repeated at Schloss Ettersburg, the summer residence of Anna Amalia, the role of Pylades was taken by Karl August. In both productions the Iphigenia was Corona Schröter, a singer who had first attracted Goethe's notice in Leipzig and whom he invited to Weimar as *Kammersängerin* (officially appointed concert-singer) to the Dowager Duchess.

[2] Quoted in Emil Schaffer, *Goethe's äussere Erscheinung. Literarische und Künstlerische Dokumente seiner Zeitgenossen* (Leipzig, 1914).

Corona Schröter made her debut on the Weimar stage as Sophie in *Partners in Guilt* (9 January 1777), subsequently appearing as Lila, as Mandandane in *The Triumph of Sensibility* and as Dortchen in *The Fisher Girl*—a play whose opening ballad *The Erl-King* she set to music. But amongst her many roles, Iphigenia was undoubtedly her greatest. She possessed the same 'union of physical and spiritual beauty' which Hufeland observed in Goethe himself. Like Frau von Stein she was a kindred spirit to him and her influence was strongly felt, not only in the Amateur Theatre but in the Professional Court Theatre later, where she was used to train young actresses. Tribute to her talent is paid in Goethe's poem *On Mieding's Death*:

> Draw gently back, dear friends, and clear a space.
> See who approaches now with solemn pace!
> Inspiring fount of virtue, it is she:
> The Muses send us their own emissary.
> You know her well, her charm's undying power—
> She graces all creation like a flower.
> Yet petal's beauty is the mere reflection
> Of what has grown, in her, to be perfection.
> The Muses mingled offerings in her heart,
> Nature, herself, in her created art.
> Here all allurement finds a welcome place:
> Your very name, Corona, crowns your grace.

The presence of Corona was undoubtedly an inspiration to the other actors, as must have been that of Ekhof when he was invited back to Weimar to appear with the amateurs in a production of *The West Indian* by Cumberland in 1778. Ekhof took the role of Stockwell and Goethe played his son. Thus the founder of the Schwerin Academy, 'the Father of German Acting', came together on the stage with the founder of Weimar Classicism.

The presence of Ekhof, if only for one production, reminds us that the Amateur Theatre was in many ways the equivalent of the best professional theatre of its time. Certainly in the care with which it studied its texts and conducted its rehearsals it was superior to many of the *Wandertruppen*. In matters of costuming, choreography and scenic construction it could call on professional aid. The Court Dancing-Master, Aulhorn, the painter, Schuhmann, and the all-important tailors, Hauenschild and Thiele, were always to hand. So, too, was the Master of Music, Wolff, whose services were needed both as composer (failing the contributions of Corona Schröter or Anna Amalia) and musical director. But most important of all was Johann Mieding, the Court-joiner:

> . . . the man who never failed.
> Ingeniously and with an anxious heart
> He solved all problems of the joiner's art.
> The scaffold which his skill did not inspire
> Swayed like a skeleton on lifeless wire.
> . . . .
> The lords and ladies often fill the hall,
> The orchestra strikes up, the prompter's call
> Is knocked three times, yet still the heights he scales,
> Bears wood, pulls ropes, and knocks in final nails.
> . . . .
> All beauty that might gentle hearts engage
> Was truly simulated on his stage:
> The green of lawns, the water's silver fall,
> The thunder's mighty crack, the songbird's call,
> An arbour's gloom, or moonlight clear and pale—
> Why, even monsters could not make him quail!
>
> As Nature's self will strive to coalesce
> Vexatious powers and opposites redress,
> So went to work his keen industrious hand:
> The poet's world arose at his command.
>
> *(On Mieding's Death)*

Many of the devices alluded to in the above lines were constructed by Mieding and others for the performance of *The Triumph of Sensibility*. 'The green of lawns' was normally the province of Schuhmann, the painter, but as we have seen this play called for the boxes of 'travelling nature' to transform themselves into rocks and grass-seats. Accordingly we find in Mieding's account for 6 February 1778 that he provided '4 frames for free-standing rocks and 2 grass-seats'. Five stage-hands, doubtless in costume, were required to achieve the transformation scene. The arbour, which had to be carried round the stage in the second act by four Moors, was also constructed by him, having on the top of it 'a machine for moonlight' that was equipped with two 'wings' and could be turned with the aid of a 'large wheel and 1 crank'. This was clearly an elaborate piece of machinery which produced the contrast between the 'arbour's gloom' and 'moonlight clear and pale'. The waterfall in this play called for similar ingenuity and for this Mieding constructed 'a contrivance with 4 cranks'. Wooden piping 'covered with sheets of metal with holes like a grater' also assisted in the illusion, as did the glass for the waterfall specially cut by Rode, the glass-master. But perhaps Mieding's greatest achievement for this production was the 'life-sized doll' in whose bosom the works of sensibility had to be discovered, and who was required by the script to resemble exactly the actress playing Mandandane. It had seven pounds of stuffing inside it, was wired in arms and legs, had its wig dressed by the Court hairdresser, and was opened by means of 'a spring with 2 wooden screws'.

Many of the performances took place in the house of Hauptmann, Master of the Ducal Game, who was also a building contractor and had built his residence with the intention of hiring it out for masked balls. Mieding was called on, therefore, to erect a portable stage in this building whenever performances took place. Initially this stage was small, having a front curtain 6.16 m. wide × 3.92 m. high and a backcloth 4.20 m. wide × 3.36 m. high. By 1776 the dimensions of the stage had been enlarged so that the backcloth for *The West Indian* measured 5.60 m. wide × 4.20 m. high.[3] The conditions of performance

[3] These dimensions are given by Gisela Sichardt, *Das Weimarer Liebhabertheater unter Goethes Leitung* (Arion Verlag, Weimar, 1957), pp. 15-16, together with details of Mieding's accounts etc.

certainly made it impossible in the early days for chariot-machinery[4] to be employed under the stage for scene changes. The Court Theatre which had burned down in 1774 had possessed such machinery, and since Mieding had worked with the Seyler–Ekhof company he would have been familiar with it, but evidence that he ever introduced it in the theatre in Hauptmann's house is inconclusive. Despite a single reference in the records to a *Wagen* (possibly a chariot but equally possibly a piece of movable scenery *on* stage, not a device for changing flats from below) the permanent floor of Hauptmann's ballroom would scarcely have allowed for a deep under-stage area. In *The West Indian* we know that scene changes were made by means of *Klappkulissen*. These were flats that were nailed to the floor (three on each side of the stage) and covered with a double layer of canvas. The upper layer was stitched to the lower across the middle of the flat, the sides being left loose and attached to rods. Strings from these rods were then fastened at the back of the flat. Thus the upper layer could be either exposed in its entirety, or flapped up or down, to produce three different changes of scene. Needless to say, the nailing of flats to the stage was ruinous to the floor-boards in the course of time, and Mieding's accounts make it clear that they had to be frequently renewed.

Lighting effects were ambitious. For *Lila* a means of lowering the footlights into a trap was achieved, so that comparative darkness could be simulated. The description of *The Fisher Girl* already given reveals how conscious Goethe was of the effect of light in dramatic performances. Twenty-one extra light-holders are recorded as having been supplied for *The Triumph of Sensibility* and four special 'Theatre lamps' for *Lila*. When Hauptmann's business failed and he was forced to sell his house to President von Kalb, Anna Amalia provided a new theatre in her own palace: here the back of the stage was furnished with two large doors which were apparently intended

---

[4] For a description of continental 'chariots' see Richard Southern, *The Seven Ages of Theatre* (Faber, 1962), pp. 221–30.

AMATEUR THEATRE AT WEIMAR

to be opened to reveal firework displays against a natural background.

Since performances took place not only in the town but also, amongst other places, in Anna Amalia's summer residence of Ettersburg, all scenery and machines had to be easily transportable. As *Mieding's Death* reminds us, the audiences might find themselves

> In huts confined, in halls of rich delight,
> In Tiefurt's vale, on Ettersburg's tall height,
> In flimsy tents, on carpets fit for kings,
> Beneath the span of night's exalted wings.

The total organisation of the enterprise was therefore complicated. Yet though Goethe was the central figure of it all, there is no evidence that he was in any way dictatorial—a charge sometimes made against his conduct of the Professional Theatre later on. Not only did he leave much free responsibility to men like Mieding and Aulhorn, he also allowed the actors considerable freedom. In *The Triumph of Sensibility*, for example, we find the stage direction:

Andrason produces a scroll from his belt and unrolls it. The young ladies approach him in turn, read, laugh and make their observations. It is up to the wit and humour of the actresses concerned to play this gaily and pleasantly and for that reason it is left to them to improvise. (Act I)

Goethe himself played Andrason on this occasion and the actresses in question included Minna von Kalb, Amalia von Lyncker (daughter of the President of the Upper Consistory Council) and Caroline von Ilten (whose beauty Prince Constantin so greatly admired). The natural grace and intelligence of these ladies perhaps allowed Goethe to direct them in the theatre more freely than the professional actresses who came later. They were, like him, well educated and full of idealism— accordingly he felt he could trust their taste; he knew they would resist the stereotyped acting that was so often to be found among the professionals and which he, himself, guyed in the same performance:

(Soft Music.)
(Andrason goes through the stereotyped movements by which actors customarily represent sensibility.) (Act I)

Even so, the casts of the plays—which included such works as a version of *The Barber of Seville*, adaptations of Aristophanes' *The Birds* and Gozzi's *Fortunate Beggar* as well as translations of *The Clandestine Marriage* and *Le Médecin malgré lui*—were not entirely composed of aristocracy. Almost everybody connected with the Court seems to have taken part at some time or other— from Anna Amalia and Frau Stein (who made her single appearance as Miss Russport in the first production of *The West Indian*) down to Mieding who came on to the stage as the candle-snuffer in *The Fair at Plundersweilen*.

The last performance by the Amateur Theatre was Gozzi's *Zobeis*, with Corona Schröter in the title role, on 21 March 1783. Goethe had been put in charge of the finances of the Duchy a year before this and his time was now too full for amateur theatricals. Three years later he was to leave for Italy, a country whose art and beauty he had longed to see. Amongst the unfinished works which he took with him were *Torquato Tasso* and *Iphigenia*, the two plays which in their final forms show the clearest influence of classicism on his theatre. Yet the real seeds of this classicism were sown at the time of the Amateur Theatre. *Iphigenia* demonstrates this conclusively. Goethe's task in Italy was merely to re-cast it in verse. Yet the pain which this apparently simple task cost him, emphasises the artistic discipline which had informed all the amateur productions. At first Goethe thought his work would be easy and he confesses as much in a letter to Herder of November 1786. But other letters to Herder and to Frau von Stein show him constantly thinking he is going to finish it 'the following day', and as constantly finding that he is making slow progress. It was not completed until January 1787 and an observation in a

83

letter to Herder of 14 October in the previous year lets us see how the remarkable achievement of the verse in *Iphigenia* came about:

It is extraordinary that a better form of expression usually seems to be intimately connected with the metre itself.

The form disciplined the initial inspiration. The days of *Sturm und Drang*, and the notion that immediate inspiration was all an artist needed, were over. From the Weimar Court with its ministerial responsibility, and its high ideals that coupled love of gaiety with taste and seriousness of purpose, came the poet who was to imbibe the beauties of Italy and marry them to German stock in such masterpieces as *Iphigenia*, *Tasso* and *Faust*.

CHAPTER FIVE

Professional Theatre at Weimar (1791—1817)

In 1787, while Goethe was still in Italy, Schiller came to Weimar on a visit to Frau von Kalb. While there he met Charlotte von Lengefeld, whom he eventually married in 1790. It was at Charlotte's house that he first met Goethe on 7 December 1788, though friendship between the two poets was not instantaneous. Goethe, having turned his back on *Sturm und Drang*, regarded the author of *The Robbers* with suspicion, and Schiller confessed to Körner that Goethe's world was not his and their ways of looking at things were totally different. Time was to change the first impressions of both. Goethe was favourably impressed by Schiller's poems *The Gods of Greece* (1788) and *The Artists* (1789) and also by his *History of the Revolt of the United Netherlands against the Spanish Government*, and used his influence to get Schiller appointed to the Chair of History at Jena University. In 1794 Schiller invited Goethe to collaborate with him in a new journal *Die Horen* (The Horae, Goddesses of the Seasons). Goethe accepted and thus began the friendship and co-operation of the two poets which contributed so much to literature and to the theatre.

Weimar Theatre Buildings

When the Amateur Theatre ceased, a professional company led by Joseph Bellomo came to Weimar and remained there

1783–91. In the town itself they performed in the ball-room of Anna Amalia's palace, the *Redoutenhaus*, which stood opposite the Dowager Duchess's residence. The stage here was 7.14 m. in width and 9.21 m. deep.[1] It had five pairs of wings which were changed by the continental chariot system. There was no flying space and backcloths had, therefore, to be rolled when drawn up, but ample back-stage room was afforded by a broad corridor which ran back from the stage itself. The illumination of the stage was achieved by twenty-six lights (which could be lowered for night effects) in the footlight trap, and a further ninety-eight lights on the wings and above the stage. The auditorium had a gallery and a raised platform for the Ducal family. The Duke provided the costumes and scenery, and members of the Court were admitted free of charge. The general public paid for their seats.

Since Bellomo's contract only allowed him to play in Weimar during six months of the year, he was forced to find another theatre during the summer. He, therefore, set up a barn-theatre in the near-by spa of Lauchstädt. Here the stage was smaller (the proscenium opening was 5.88 m. and the depth of the stage was 7.28 m.) and the general conditions considerably simpler. It was, however, possible to use the same scenery here as in Weimar and hence considerable expense was saved.

The acting standard of Bellomo's company was low—Goethe commented to the Duke in 1784 that their theatrical offerings had descended to a state of torpor—and in 1791 Bellomo was dismissed and Goethe created 'Artistic Director of the Theatre with unrestricted powers'. Franz Kirms, Assessor to the Court Chamberlain, was appointed to take care of financial arrangements and an actor from Prague, F. J. Fischer, initially engaged to direct the plays. The new enterprise inherited both the theatres used by Bellomo. It was financially essential to keep the summer season at Lauchstädt, though the theatre there rapidly fell into decay. In 1799, one of the company, Becker, reported to Goethe:

[1] Sichardt, *op. cit*, p. 31.

Our theatre here in Lauchstädt is so miserably provided that rain comes in, not only on the stage but on the audience as well. When it rains it is quite impossible for us to remain in the men's dressing-room.[2]

Accordingly Goethe had the theatre repaired and reopened with a gala performance in 1802. The improvement was, however, only partial, for a letter from Schiller headed 'Lauchstädt, 6 July 1803', informed him:

The theatre-building has revealed to me in this short time its advantages and also its drawbacks. As far as the last are concerned, I find the voices lose their clarity, and in particular the roof, because of its form and thin construction, is too exposed to the weather. In *The Bride of Messina* a thunder-storm broke out, bringing a great deal of water which beat so heavily on the roofing that for whole quarters of an hour together not a single coherent speech could be understood, however hard the actors strove with their voices. And on the following day when I looked at the empty theatre, the ugly stains of the rain which had come in were perceptible on the beautifully painted ceiling.

But expenses had to be cut to a minimum in Weimar and not much could be spared for the summer theatre, where the audience comprised chiefly spa-guests and students from the near-by University of Halle. The latter were particularly troublesome, especially during the cherry season, when they ate fruit in the stalls and bombarded the actors with the stones. Having done so during a performance of *The Robbers* in 1799, they went on, Becker reports, to applaud every exit of one actress 'with the whistling hisses used in Halle to attract daughters of joy'.[2]

The theatre in Weimar was re-built during the summer of 1798. The stage was enlarged and the auditorium included a balcony and gallery, with separate boxes on balcony level for the Duke and Schiller. Goethe's box was under the Duke's on the ground floor. Chairs with arms now replaced the benches

[2] Letter to Goethe, 28 July 1799. Quoted by Pasqué, *op. cit.*, Vol. II, pp. 152–61.

of the old theatre and the audience was seated according to rank: middle class and students downstairs, courtiers and officials in the balcony and the populace in the gallery. As each paying patron entered, he surrendered his ticket and received a contra-ticket. The Controller put the original in a sealed box, while the contra-ticket was given up to an usher and put into his own sealed box—the contents of both boxes being checked in the box-office in the interval.

In the new theatre oil lamps replaced the tallow candles of the old and the auditorium was partially darkened by raising the largest chandelier into an opening in the ceiling. Possibly the eighteen wall-lights on the pillars of the stalls were extinguished during performance, but lights in the balcony and gallery remained on. The main curtain was lowered only at the end of the acts: scenery and furniture were changed for individual scenes in full view of the audience, and for this reason furniture was kept to a minimum. Simplicity was always the keynote of Weimar productions and even in plays like *Wallenstein* whole armies were represented by a handful of soldiers, in contrast to the spectacular crowds assembled on the Berlin stage by Iffland in his productions of Schiller.

Goethe describes the interior decoration of the 1798 theatre as being 'in the best taste: serious but not heavy, splendid without being overcharged'.[3] The style was neo-classical; Doric pillars painted to resemble antique marble with bronzed capitals were surmounted by masks representing tragic and comic subjects. Thus the whole became a fitting framework for the style of acting and production which Goethe inspired.

Weimar style

The distinctive mixture of 'classical' and 'romantic' ideals at the heart of Weimar style (both in the plays and in the methods used to realise them on stage) is revealed by *What We Offer*, an allegorical piece written by Goethe for the reopening of the

[3] Quoted by Kindermann, *op. cit.*, vol. V (1962), p. 184.

Lauchstädt theatre in 1802. Here the God Mercury visits an old couple, who might have stepped out of a German folk-tale and whose dilapidated dwelling represents:

> . . . our former theatre, which so often
> Has vexed both you and us in days that now are passed
> With its discomforts.

There is even a carpet hung up to the ceiling purporting to catch drips of rain. Mercury and the old man fly away on this carpet to a 'splendid hall' (the symbol of the new theatre) where various allegorical figures expound the ideals of neo-classic art. The theme of the play is the apparent conflict between Art (illusion) and Nature (reality) and its action, Mercury explains to us, symbolises the actors' desire to reach 'the higher regions of our noble art'. One of the characters, however, the old lady, openly refuses to be an allegorical figure:

I'm a good simple woman and I intend to remain so and be taken for what I am.   (Scene XVII)

In order to emphasise the difference between Art and Nature, Goethe deliberately allows her to speak sometimes as a 'character' and sometimes as the actress playing that character. At the end of the play the conflict between the two worlds is shown to be resolved when an artist masters the techniques of his trade so well that all sense of artifice disappears. The resultant, highly disciplined effect seems perfectly 'natural', yet at the same time is subtly contrived to highlight the Truth that lies beyond mere appearance:

> Nature and Art seem opposites in vain:
> Ere we're aware they're reconciled at heart.
> I feel my own aversions, too, depart—
> Both to affection have an equal claim.
>
> Nothing avails but honest toil and pain
> And if we first give measured hours to Art,
> Surrendering her our industry and heart—
> Why, Nature's freedom glows in us again!

> Thus, only, is the Truth revealed as whole.
> Unfettered spirits vainly seek to paint
> Perfection's pure supernal majesty.
>
> Who would be great must martial up his soul:
> The master is revealed in his restraint,
> And law alone can make us truly free.   (Scene XIV)

The statement that 'The master is revealed in his restraint' is
a measure of the difference between the Goethe of *Götz von
Berlichingen* and the mature dramatist of the later plays. If those
later plays and the great verse tragedies of Schiller were to be
realised on the Weimar stage, however, Goethe knew that his
actors had to be trained to the task. Some were the merest
beginners, some had been inherited from Bellomo's company,
some from other companies. The first essential, therefore, was to
weld them into an *ensemble*—a point which he stressed in the
Prologue he wrote to inaugurate the Court Theatre on 7 May
1791:

> The start of every enterprise is stubborn:
> . . . .
> We might presume, all we assembled here,
> To uncover facets of the actor's art
> By individual skill. . . .
> Yet we reflect that Harmony alone,
> Sustained throughout the play, deserves your praise.
> So let each player suit his partner's vein
> And all together offer you a whole
> Complete in Beauty. . . .
> No single individual shall strive
> To outstrip his neighbour, and with breathless haste
> Greedily snatch the laurel for himself.

To prevent selfish 'star' performances, Goethe arranged that
the type of roles given to each player was constantly varied.
All were required to appear as 'supers' if no leading part was
available. His greatest task, however, was to train them in the
speaking of verse. The natural flow of poetic language in plays

like *Wallenstein* and *Iphigenia* was something totally new to German theatre. The translations made by Gottsched had been, as we have seen, stiff and rhetorically turgid; Lessing's plays, with the exception of *Nathan* which was not performed until 1783, were in prose, so too were the *Sturm und Drang* works of Goethe and Schiller. Thus the speaking of great verse by German actors had to be learned. To this end Goethe gave classes to the younger members of the company (numbering roughly twelve) in verse speaking and other aspects of the style required in poetic tragedy. From these classes came *The Rules for Actors*, originally noted down by Pius Alexander Wolff and Franz Grüner about the year 1803 and published by Eckermann in 1826. Since Goethe's enemies—notably the actor Karl Reinhold, who failed to get lasting employment at Weimar—have attacked his precepts so bitterly, it must be stressed that the *Rules* do not represent a philosophy of the art of acting, but rather a series of notes for the specific purpose of training a particular group of actors in a particular style. Hence hardly any mention is made of comic acting—except in so far as Rule 91 points out that comic style is the opposite of all that has gone before. Hence, too, the fact that general principles rub shoulders with more trivial, but practical, matters such as the injunction that: 'Young ladies must leave their little handbags on one side when actually rehearsing.'

The first two rules are concerned with 'Dialect'—an important matter at Weimar since, as the Prologue for 7 May 1791 pointed out, the company came 'from every end of Germany'. Even Schiller retained a strong Swabian dialect all his days. It was clearly undesirable to have conflicting regional accents in high tragedy, however, and hence the first of Goethe's rules lays it down that: 'No provincialism shall raise its head on the stage.' He goes on to demand particular attention to word-endings and proper names. Such virtues, no doubt, could be exaggerated and Reinhold in his pamphlet *Seeds sown by Goethe* (1808) complains that they were. Yet it was not Goethe's intention to produce stilted delivery, as Rule 5 explains:

Speech is pure when all the words are so pronounced that the sense takes hold of the listener easily and distinctly.

The sense—the intention of the poet as expressed in the text—was of paramount importance, but Nature's freedom was to glow in the 'ease' with which the actor expressed it. To this end the many reading rehearsals were directed, where Goethe himself took part, giving on one occasion a particularly impressive and well-characterised delivery of Shakespeare's Falstaff.[4] Reinhold's criticism that characterisation was lacking in Weimar productions, that 'Father and son, old man and young, man and wife' spoke and acted with monotonous uniformity will not ultimately hold water. In the first place it is contradicted by the opinions of others. Writing of Christiane Neumann, the child actress whom Goethe and Corona Schröter trained, Iffland observed: 'If she carries on the same way for some years, Germany will have no other actress.'[5] Pius Alexander Wolff, of whom Goethe once said he was the only man 'who has formed himself from the ground up totally according to the spirit I taught him', was praised by the dramatist Adolph Müllner for his powerful and easy delivery of lines. And so on. In the second place, Reinhold's position as an actor who had failed to gain favour at Weimar, makes him a suspect witness.

The same must be said of Madame Burgdorf, a temperamental and troublesome actress who was engaged after the early death of Christiane Neumann. Of the intrigues of Burgdorf and her so-called 'husband', the curious reader may find lengthy evidence in Pasqué.[6] Suffice it here to say that Goethe's initial judgement of her in a letter to Kirms —'I don't mind betting the woman has never been on the stage and is a worthless wretch'[7]—was substantially correct. Too much credence, therefore, cannot be given to her complaint in a letter to Goethe

---

[4] See Genast, *Aus dem Tagebuch eines alten Schauspielers*, p. 53f.
[5] Quoted by Pasqué, *op. cit.*, vol. I, p. 101.
[6] See Pasqué, *op. cit.*, vol. I, pp. 179–252.
[7] Letter to Kirms 19 September 1778.

(15 December 1798) that her expression of feeling on the stage was forced to bear 'the imprint of a borrowed stamp', that her declamation suffered 'the fetters of an unaccustomed rhythm' and that she became 'a machine moved by alien dictates'. Exaggeration was always the characteristic of Madame Burgdorf's epistles and several instances in the *Rules* show that a 'machine' was the last thing Goethe wanted as an actor. Thus, Rule 77 states:

It is . . . inevitably necessary that the actor should . . . think himself in his role when it comes to performance and his mind be able to occupy itself only with the personage he has assumed.

The actor must:

. . . make the character and the whole situation to be presented completely his own. He must allow his *imagination* to work over the material properly, for without this preparation he will not be in a position either to speak or act correctly.   (64)

With this aim in mind, Goethe discouraged actors from committing their parts to memory too early: true imaginative response could only arise from careful and objective study. As a final word on this topic, we may turn to *Wilhelm Meister*. Here the company amuse themselves on one occasion by improvising the plot, lines and characters of a play. The Stranger (who speaks here for the author) observes:

I find this exercise very useful both for actors, and for friends and acquaintances in society. It is the best way to get people out of themselves and bring them back into themselves again by a different route. It ought to be introduced into every troupe. They should be compelled to exercise themselves in this way and the public would certainly be the richer if an unscripted play were to be put on once a month—though, or course, the actors would have to prepare themselves for it with several rehearsals.   (Book II, Chapter IX)

The insistence on 'several rehearsals' indicates the sharp distinction which Goethe drew between 'useful exercises' and public performances in which:

... All stiffness must vanish, all rules become the hidden guide-lines of a living action. (90)

The same passage in *Meister* relates to the sections of the *Rules* which deal with movement. The Stranger goes on to declare that improvisation is particularly relevant to the study of gesture, also making a revealing comment on the style of German acting as a whole:

There are, indeed, actors in Germany whose bodies show what they are thinking and feeling, who use silence, hesitation, gestures and gracefully gentle movements of the body to prepare a speech, understanding how to unite the pauses of a dialogue to the whole by means of a pleasing mime. But an exercise which would help an instinctive actor and teach him how to vie with the writer is much to be desired. It is not so frequently employed as the patrons of the theatre might wish. (*Ibid.*)

The *Rules* also recommend that a young actor should go through his part entirely in mime to begin with, trying to express the full meaning by gesture only, 'since then he is compelled to choose the most suitable movements' (65). The object of gesture is always 'to paint the meaning, but in such a way that it seems instinctive' (55). Reinhold, however, would have us believe that the actors were 'only allowed to speak, but never act'. One can only observe that the *Rules* give a quite different impression: they begin with the statement that 'the art of the actor consists in speech and bodily movement', and roughly 40 out of the total 91 concern themselves with movement.

Goethe's attitude to action on the stage embodies a mixture of the aesthetic and the socially correct, which is different in some respects from theories held in the previous century by such actors as Betterton.[8] Betterton's attitude to gesture, when not concerned with it as a means of characterisation, is predominantly occupied with propriety. Actors must never make use of any 'lewd, obscene or indecent posture'. They must never, at

[8] See *Life of Mr. Thomas Betterton* by Gildon (1710).

least in Tragedy, adopt 'the Posture of one *bending a Bow*, presenting a *Musquet*, or playing on any Musical Instrument, as if you had it in your hands'. Most characteristically of all, Betterton declares that it is *indecent* to make a gesture with the left hand alone, the underlying assumption presumably being that left-handedness was an exception to the Divine Law of Nature.

Goethe assumes a symbolic rather than a 'natural' significance in the use of the right hand and the right side of the stage. 'Persons who are to be accorded respect—young ladies, the elderly and the nobly born' are always to be placed on the right of the scene (42). In considering gestures with the right hand, he takes a quite different view from Betterton:

If I have to stretch out my hand and the right is not specifically demanded, I can just as well give the left: for on the stage neither right not left has any special validity: one must always aim not to destroy the picture that is to be presented by disturbing movements.

(58)

For Goethe 'the picture to be presented' is the prime consideration. He was not like Betterton, Garrick and Iffland, an actor-manager who appeared in his own productions. He was one of the first 'modern' directors, whose function was clearly separated from that of the actor and who could, therefore, take a more objective view of the whole. He co-ordinated not only the actors' response to the text, but the groupings on the stage. Here symmetry was all important to him, as repeated insistence in the stage directions of Weimar plays reminds us. Actors were not to play too near the wings, nor were they to pass beyond the proscenium line (85). In general, he favoured diagonal moves rather than perpendicular ones, and actors were invited to make a sketch of the stage divided up like a draught-board, in order that they might work out for themselves where their most suitable positions might be (87). Thus, one notices the sense of responsibility which he allows the actor. How far this was justified in all cases is another matter. Rule 35 declares:

95

First and foremost the actor must be aware that he must not only imitate nature, he must represent her ideally, and therefore unite Truth with Beauty in his performance.

Other rules, however, reveal a need to teach propriety to the raw recruits of the company, as in the section headed:

Bad Habits to be Avoided

Amongst the most uncouth faults which are to be avoided must be counted that of an actor who is seated and in order to bring his chair further forward thrusts his hands down between his thighs, grabs hold of the seat, raises himself somewhat, and so brings the chair downstage. This is not only an offence against beauty, but even more against decent behaviour.

74.

The actor will be careful not to let his handkerchief appear on stage, nor will he blow his nose, far less spit. . . . .

Reading such observations we understand why Goethe found it difficult to deal with some professional actors, who lacked the intelligence and refinement of the players he had directed in the Amateur Theatre. His favourites—Christiane Neumann and Wolff—were exceptional cases. (The first was a child who naturally took instruction, the second the son of a book-seller with some education and sensibility.) Though Goethe constantly endeavoured to improve the social standing of actors and invited them to his house, he did not find them easy companions. Breaches of discipline were met with stern measures. A contract prepared for the troublesome Burgdorfs laid it down that they should separate if Herr Burgdorf continued to create public scandals by assaulting his 'wife'. Actors who missed their cues were fined and no appeal was allowed. One member of the company who absented herself for a week was punished on her return by being confined to her quarters under military guard. Although such extreme measures are not hinted at in the *Rules*, something of Goethe's impatience with the inept and slovenly shows itself in his more mechanical prescriptions: the beginner should always start his speeches on a low note (30); and the body should always be held erect, the chest out, upper arm pressed to the side, the head slightly turned to the person addressed (37). Such directions suggest that gentle reason and persuasion sometimes failed. But there are many instances in the letters of men like Haide and Wolff that show how tolerant and humane Goethe could be. Actors were poorly paid in Weimar, yet they considered it an honour to be there, and under Goethe's direction the theatre became one of the most illustrious in the whole of Germany.

After the death of Schiller (1805), Goethe's regime became less flexible. Schiller had always found communication with the company easier, though passages in his correspondence suggest that he too could be wearied. A letter from him to Goethe on 31 August 1798, for example, agrees with the former's opinion that

. . .even good actors are, at best, only channels or reporters of the written text.

—and a further letter of 28 April 1801 declares:

I want nothing more to do with the tribe of actors, for reason and kindness can achieve nothing; there is only one relationship with them—the brusque imperative, which I have not to use.

Particularly troublesome to Goethe was Karoline Jagemann who became the mistress of Karl August. Though a talented and much admired performer, she was a difficult colleague. The climax of her machinations came when she ordered a performance of the play *Aubry de Mont-Didier's Dog or The Wood at Bondy* in April 1817 during Goethe's temporary absence in Jena. The leading role in this piece was given to a performing poodle and since Goethe had striven so long to raise the cultural level of the stage and to bring the social status of actors above that of circus animals, he was deeply affronted. He wrote a letter to the Duke resigning his position in the theatre and from 1817–28 (when Karl August died) Karoline Jagemann

97

virtually directed the theatre through the agency of her friend, Strohmeyer.

Goethe's Plays for the Professional Theatre

In view of the difficulty which the speaking of verse presented to the actors (even Schiller's *Don Carlos* being performed in prose on 25 September 1791 at Erfurt) it is not surprising that Goethe's first play for the Court Theatre was a prose comedy: *The Great Cophta* (November 1791). It is based on the affair of Marie Antoinette's diamond necklace which the trial of 1786 had made common knowledge. The historical events of the intrigue, so far as they were ever established, are closely followed but the characters are given other names. Cardinal Rohan becomes 'The Canon' who believes the Princess (Marie Antoinette) to be in love with him. Comtesse Lamotte is turned into 'The Marquise' and her Niece represents Marie Lejay, the girl who impersonated the French Queen and presented the gullible Rohan with a rose as a token of her love.

When the play opens the Canon is in disgrace and the Marquise persuades him he can regain the Princess's favour by buying a diamond necklace in her name—this service to be done as witness of his devotion and repentance. Once the necklace is bought it is the Marquise's intention to possess it, sell the jewels and escape to England. Her plan is foiled, however, by the Knight who falls in love with her Niece and betrays the conspiracy to the law. Whereas the historical situation in France had resulted in a public trial, in the Weimar comedy all is settled with the utmost discretion in a private garden: the Marquise and her husband are arrested and the Niece sent to a monastery. The Knight who had betrayed the conspiracy is left to regret that matters had been made even as public as this:

If only I'd followed my feeling and gone straight to the Canon when I accidently discovered the plot. I might have gained a friend and a beloved and I could have enjoyed my good fortune with an easy mind. But now all is lost. . . .

... I can enjoy nothing, for I haven't acted as I should have done. Only one desire, one hope, remains to me—to console the poor girl and return her to herself and to the world.   (Act V, Sc. VIII)

Goethe's intention in the play was to point out the dangers of the revolutionary theories which were spreading from France to Germany. Accordingly the action is set not in Paris but in a nameless Court where something of the ideals of 'Humanity' pertain and hence a revolution is avoided. The Knight's speeches quoted above indicate that had he acted even more 'humanely' the *dénouement* would have been even more admirable. It is almost as though the French Court were being blamed for not acting with the high-mindedness of Iphigenia. As a political thesis, therefore, the play is somewhat naïve and illustrates Goethe's basic inability to handle themes of practical politics. Yet there is throughout an awareness of stage business and an admirably swift development of plot. The most effective moments are connected with the character of Count Rostro, the Great Cophta himself, whom Goethe modelled on Cagliostro the confidence-trickster who had deceived half Europe. He is represented as a false prophet of Free Masonry who dupes the Court into believing him a God. His pre-arranged 'magic' is accompanied by a refreshing affrontery. He claims, for example, to be able to command spirits to open doors and, when the illusion has been successfully performed, has the following dialogue with one of the Canon's servants:

Saint Jean (*who enters with care*) : Did I not do my part of the business well?
Count: You fulfilled your duty.
Saint Jean: Didn't the doors fly open as if they'd been burst apart by spirits? . . .
Count: . . . I could have managed to open them without your help—except, of course, that such an operation requires more trouble. I often have to take refuge in vulgar methods, so as not to incommode the noble spirits all the time.   (Act I, Sc. V)

Stage directions throughout are copious and detailed—a   99 marked contrast to the *Iphigenia* which had been written for the Amateurs. Speeches are prefaced by such observations as:

Half aloud, as though he were speaking to himself, but so that the Canon can hear it. (Act III, Sc. III)

and

Recognises her and expresses his horror in mime. (Act V, Sc. VIII)

Careful attention is also paid to aesthetically satisfying grouping:

The main characters press round her, the young men come upstage from the proscenium line, the children join them fearfully. They all form a beautiful but informal group. (Act III, Sc. IX)

He throws himself at the Niece's feet. She leans on the Marquise. The Marquis stands by disconcertedly and they make an attractive group on the right side of the stage in which the two Swiss soldiers are not to be forgotten. The Colonel and two other Swiss guards stand on the left side of the stage. (Act V, Sc. VI)

Two other plays on themes suggested by the French Revolution were also written at this time: the unfinished *The Agitators* (1793) and *The Citizen-General* of the same year. *The Citizen-General*, a one-act comedy, was written as a sequel to two plays by Anton Wall in which the actor Beck had had a great success. Here again it is Goethe's intention to show how disciplined common sense and tactful sensibility can avoid the misery of revolution. The central figure (written for Beck) is Schnaps, a lovable rogue who steals the uniform of a French prisoner of war and proceeds to rob the gullible Märten under the guise of giving him a lesson in democratic principles. Objects in the old man's house are used to demonstrate his thesis: the milk-pot becomes a fortress, the ladle stands for the citizens who must storm the fort and the cream represents the aristocracy that must be 'skimmed off' into Schnaps's stomach. Such commotion is created that neighbours summon the law and Schnapps only avoids arrest by the intervention of a passing nobleman who points out the moral of the play:

. . . Ill-timed laws and punishments only produce trouble. In a land where the Prince is aware of all men's needs, where all classes think fairly of each other and each may be productive in his own way . . . no parties will arise. . . .

It says a lot for us that we can laugh for a moment at this cockade, cap and uniform which have brought such evil to the world.

(Scene XIV)

The Court Theatre's Repertoire

In his essay *Weimar Court Theatre* (1802) Goethe states his intention 'to build up a repertory that could be left to posterity', at the same time recognising that this necessarily meant educating the taste of the public. On occasions his efforts to do this met with opposition—as when titters broke out in the audience during a performance of a play by Friedrich Schlegel and had to be silenced by the famous command from Goethe's box 'Do not laugh!' Through the years, however, in addition to the dramas of Goethe and Schiller, an ambitious repertoire of plays and operas was established, which set an example to other theatres and is in no small way responsible for the internationally orientated programme of German civic theatres today.

In the operatic field Mozart was a favourite. *Il Seraglio* was given in Goethe's first season as Director and the following year saw Goethe's production of *Don Giovanni*—an opera repeated nearly every year during his tenure of office and numbering 68 performances. Within two years of its premiere in Prague, *The Magic Flute* was performed, though few other German theatres had ventured to present it. *Cosi fan Tutte* and *Titus* followed in 1797 and 1799 respectively. Beethoven's *Fidelio* joined the repertoire in 1816, two years after the first Weimar production of *Egmont* to use Beethoven's music.

In non-musical drama the contemporary German scene was represented, amongst others, by Kotzebue (a native of Weimar

101

whose melodramas had made him famous throughout Europe, Sheridan adapting one of his plays in 1799) and by Iffland, whose plays were of the sentimental school. Besides these Goethe set more serious offerings. Having learned of the new and more 'natural' style of acting introduced by Talma in France, he turned to French plays which could afford his own company opportunity of learning this mixture of naturalism and classic discipline, and adapted Voltaire's *Mahomet* (1800) and *Tancred* (1801). French theatre was further represented by Racine's *Mithridate* (1804) and Schiller's adaptation of *Phèdre* in blank verse (1805). In 1806 Corneille's *Le Cid* was performed.

In 1808 Talma came to Weimar, having been brought to perform in Erfurt by Napoleon, who admired his talent so greatly that he wished to show him off to the various kings of Europe assembled for the Erfurt Conference. His visit impressed not only Goethe but also Pius Alexander Wolff who copied his style of acting in Calderon's *The Constant Prince* (1811). The next year Calderon's *Life's a Dream* was performed and in 1815 his *Zenobia*. Thus Spanish drama, too, came to Weimar, while Italy was represented both by Goldoni (a long-standing favourite with the audiences) and by Schiller's verse adaptation of Gozzi's prose play *Turandot*, in which Commedia dell'arte influence was thus mingled with Weimar classicism.

Classical dramas also had their place and Goethe's use of half-masks for Terence's *The Brothers* (1801) is noteworthy. As an experiment he had used masks for his own occasional-piece *Paläophron and Neoterpe* at a private Court performance a year earlier, but their use in the public theatre was unheard of at that time and even nineteenth-century critics like Lewes failed to see the merit of such an academic approach.

In view of the catholicity and imagination of the whole programme, it is sad to have to report that one of Goethe's big failures was the world premiere of Kleist's *The Broken Jug* (1808). This classic comedy of the German stage, performed in England in the twentieth century by Sir Donald Wolfit and well known to international audiences by the film with Emil

Jannings, lay outside the confines of Weimar style. It required a coarser realism, and Goethe's unfortunate division of it into three acts slowed the development of the plot. But if Kleist failed, the production of Zacharias Werner's *24th. February* (1810) revealed that the company could well adapt themselves to the Romantic style of the so-called Fate Drama—as might have been expected from the Romantic style of certain of their Shakespeare productions.

Shakespeare at Weimar

The first Shakespearian play to be given by the Court Theatre was *King John* in 1791, directed by Goethe himself and translated into prose by Eschenburg. This somewhat unusual choice is explained by Goethe's desire to create a theatrical event worthy of the first season of his Directorship: the play had never been performed in Germany before and in the child actress, Christiane Neumann, he realised he had a Prince Arthur of distinction. His hopes in her were not disappointed. The play, he reports, was 'our greatest financial success and Christiane Neumann . . . whom I had instructed myself, made the most wonderful impression. My task had to be to bring the rest of the company into harmony with her.'[9]

The following year on 28 January *Hamlet* was presented and proudly advertised on the bill as being 'completely according to the Original'. The translation was again by Eschenburg and the claim to authenticity is worth noting. Even some of Garrick's productions of Shakespeare in England were far from the original texts: the Grave-digger was left out of *Hamlet*, *Lear* was performed in Nahum Tate's version which allowed Cordelia to survive and marry Edgar, and the dying Romeo was allowed to speak to Juliet on her awakening. It is not, therefore, surprising that the German stage, with its inheritance of versions like the *Brudermord* and dependence upon translation,

[9] Quoted by Pasqué, *op. cit.*, vol. I, p. 100.

H

took considerable time in achieving 'genuine' Shakespeare. It was not until Schröder staged his version of *Hamlet* in Hamburg (20 September 1776) that anything approaching a true text was attained. Even so, this text was not apparently sufficiently authentic for Goethe in 1792, although it was probably Schröder's version which inspired the staging of *Hamlet* by the Wandering Players in the novel *Wilhelm Meister*. What is clear from the novel is the daring of the whole enterprise— Shakespeare is 'discovered' both by the players and Meister himself.

A thoroughly satisfactory version of *Hamlet* did not appear in Germany until Schlegel's[10] translation, staged by Iffland in Berlin on 15 October 1799. This remarkable achievement, which succeeded in making the translated text sound like original German verse and has remained the 'standard' theatrical text in Germany to this day, was adopted by Weimar for later productions. As Hamlet, Pius Alexander Wolff achieved one of his greatest successes and his scene with the Ghost was particularly admired. He was even allowed, contrary to the rules of Goethe's stage, to turn his back to the audience in this passage and express his emotion through the trembling of his hands and body.

A first performance of one of Schlegel's translations, *Julius Caesar*, was presented by Goethe in 1803. Once more the language is remarkably easy and proved itself successful on the Weimar stage. Previous to this, Goethe had staged *Henry IV* in 1792 (the first German production of the play in two parts) and *King Lear* (in Schröder's version but without the 'happy-ending' which Schröder had been forced to use in Berlin and Mannheim in order to attract audiences).

In May 1800 Schiller's adaptation of *Macbeth* was produced. It was undoubtedly the finest translation of the play which existed in Germany at that time and, since Schlegel did not attempt the piece, became the standard German text until

---

[10] August Wilhelm Schlegel—not to be confused with Friedrich Schlegel mentioned above.

well into the nineteenth century. (When Ludwig Tieck completed Schlegel's translations of the Shakespeare canon, he unfortunately gave *Macbeth* to his daughter to translate and the work is not satisfactory.) Since it was essentially Goethe's and Schiller's intention to present Shakespeare as a 'classic' dramatist, rather than as the 'lawless' genius whom they had extolled in the days of *Sturm und Drang*, certain changes were made in the text. To begin with everything, including even Lady Macbeth's sleep-walking scene, is rendered into verse. Thus the desired new 'harmony' of the whole was achieved—though Schiller generally stays close to the original prose meaning. Thus, in some respects, this versification of the whole does not amount to more than the kind of stylistic interpretation which modern directors sometimes impose on a text. The Porter appears but his dialogue at 'hell's gate' is replaced by a song. This opens in lyrical style but goes on to warn us that

> What was hidden in the night
> Will be discovered by day's light. (*Loud Knocking.*)
> . . . .
> And many a man scarce shuts his eyes
> Yet does not see the sun arise.
> Therefore rejoice all you who gaze
> Alive upon the morning rays!
> (*He opens the door. Macduff and Ross enter.*)   (Act II, Sc. V)

Thus lyricism mixed with dramatic irony replace the earthiness of the Porter's bawdy. But the essential point of the Shakespearean humour at this juncture is not entirely overlooked by Schiller. He supplies a passage of riddle-dialogue which is at least an attempt at Shakespeare-pastiche, though it lacks the pungency of the original observations on the effects of drink.

Ross: . . . Thou hast so strong an organ in thy breast
         That thou mightst blast all Scotland from its slumber.
Porter: I could, indeed, Sir. Am I not the man
         Who guarded Scotland for you through this night?   105

Ross: How so, friend Porter?

Porter: Why, Sir, it is thus:
Does not the King keep watch on all his people?
And is it not the Porter's watch which keeps
The King protected through the night? And thus,
You see that I have watched the whole of Scotlar.d. (*Ibid.*)

In much the same way certain passages of the Witches (whose doggerel was considered unworthy) have been expanded in order to make their function as tempters of Macbeth more clear. By and large, however, the translation is better than many critics have allowed and frequently captures the splendour of Shakespeare's original.

For his production of *Romeo and Juliet* (1812) Goethe used Schlegel's translation but with certain adaptations of his own at the beginning and end of the play. Before examining these it is important to remember that an earlier version of the play by Christian Felix Weisse had previously held the German stage. The Weisse version had followed Garrick's usage in allowing Romeo to speak with Juliet in the tomb: it was also in prose, reduced the action to two locations and observed the neo-classical unity of time. Goethe's much-criticised adaptations are nearer to Shakespeare than this—as far as the end of the play is concerned he merely cut the lengthy summary of all that has gone before by Friar Laurence, an excision which is followed by nearly all modern directors. In the opening the bustle and bawdy is removed and both the Nurse and Mercutio suffer in the process. Yet while the loss of the Queen Mab speech is severe, one can at least see some reason for Goethe's action. In any production of the play Mercutio is liable to outshine Romeo and it was, perhaps, Goethe's realisation of this that made him reduce the part. In his essay *Shakespeare and no End* he writes:

In *Romeo and Juliet*, Shakespeare ... almost destroys the tragic content of the whole by the two comic figures of the Nurse and Mercutio, who were probably played by two popular actors, the former, of course, being taken by a man. If one considers the dramatic economy of the piece exactly, one notices that these two figures . . . only come in as farcical intermezzi which must be intolerable on the stage to our logical and harmony-loving way of thought.

This passage reflects Goethe's final opinion that Shakespeare was greater as a poet than as a dramatist. It must be seen in the light of a later paragraph:

In the last few years the prejudice has crept into Germany that Shakespeare has got to be put on our stages word for word, even though actors and audiences are strangled in the attempt . . . If the defenders of this opinion get the upper hand then Shakespeare will be driven from our stages altogether. This would be no misfortune, for the reader, either single or in company, would then have the purer pleasure in him.

Goethe was by no means alone in thinking that Shakespeare gave more pleasure when read than staged—we have only to remember Charles Lamb's view of *Lear*. But he recognised the power of the plays in performance, as he also recognised the need for directors and translators to modify details that might be unacceptable to a particular audience in the cause of interesting them in the work as a whole. Goethe's *Romeo and Juliet* and Schiller's *Macbeth* were not, from the purists' point of view, Shakespeare's, but they were no further away from him than many other eighteenth-century adaptations and a good deal nearer than some. They must be judged as productions rather than scholarly texts. If men like Goethe, Garrick and Tree had not adapted Shakespeare to suit the audiences of their time, his plays would not have lived on their stages and, hence, might have been lost to ours. And in this connection it is relevant to note that the two versions of Weimar classics which have found most favour in the English-speaking theatre —Stephen Spender's *Mary Stuart* and John Arden's *Ironhand*— are both self-confessed 'adaptations'. The Weimar poets would

107

have seen the necessity for altering certain facets of their work for the sake of an audience unfamiliar with their traditions. The gulf between the ideal of 'exact' translation and the practical necessity of realising a play on stage for other periods, peoples and purposes, will never be perfectly bridged.

CHAPTER SIX

Schiller's Major Plays: His Theory and Practice

Don Carlos

Schiller began his first blank-verse tragedy, *Don Carlos*, in 1782 and part of it was published in the *Rheinische Thalia* in 1785. The complete play was not finished, however, until two years later and the dramatist observed:

During the time in which I was working on the play, which because of several interruptions was a fairly long period—a great deal had changed in myself. (*Letters on Don Carlos*, 1788, Letter 1)

As it now stands, the play presents two major themes: the love tragedy of Don Carlos, son of Philip II of Spain, and the struggle of the Netherlands to free themselves from the Spanish imperial yoke. Don Carlos is in love with Elisabeth of Valois who has been forced into marriage with his father. He mistakes a love-letter sent him by Princess Eboli, a lady-in-waiting, for one from the Queen herself. When Eboli is spurned by him she steals from the Queen the letters which Carlos had written to Elisabeth before her marriage and shows them to the King. Various and complicated intrigues ensue until Carlos is eventually arrested and a last attempt is made to save him by his friend, Marquis Posa, who tries in vain to draw suspicion upon himself.

Into the strands of this romantic plot Schiller weaves the political theme which began to interest him more and more as the play progressed. In this theme Posa and Philip are the outstanding figures. The first is the passionate advocate of freedom for the Netherlands, a man possessed by the high idealism of earlier heroes like Karl Moor and Fiesco. The second is by no means the romantic monster which Schiller found in one of the source-books he used, the *Histoire de Dom Carlos* by the Abbé St. Réal. He is a lonely figure trapped by his own despotism and only too anxious to find a friend in a man of Posa's quality. The contrast between the two men is almost as memorable as that between Mary Stuart and Elizabeth in Schiller's later play, yet here the contrast is between opposites rather than enemies and Posa's initial aim is to win the King to his side:

Marquis: O for the oratory of the thousand tongues
            That share this pregnant hour, to tremble here
            Upon my lips! The light that I perceive
            In all their eyes to burst into a flame!
            I beg of you—abandon that false godhead
            Which must destroy us! Be to us example
            Of Truth! Eternal Truth! Through all the ages
            No mortal has possessed so much, nor been
            So god-like in its dispensation. Kings
            Across all Europe honour Spain's repute.
            Then be the foremost king in Europe's span:
            One pen-stroke from your hand and all the earth
            Is new-created. Give to us our Freedom!
            Freedom of thought!—(*Throwing himself at his feet.*)
King (*overcome, turns his face away, then rivets his eyes on the Marquis again*):
                      Strange dreamer of strange dreams!
            But yet—Arise—I—
Marquis: Cast your eye upon
            God's majesty of Nature. It is grounded
            On Freedom, it is dowered by Freedom's gifts.
            The great Creator casts the tiny worm
            Within a dew-drop's compass and allows
            Unbridled instinct to find joyous life,

Even among the dead realms of decay.
How poor and how confined is your creation!
The rustling of a leaf will terrify
The Lords of Christendom and they must tremble
Before all forms of Virtue. God, to save
Despoiling Freedom's fair appearance, lets
The hideous hordes of evil freely rage.
The Heavenly Artist sits unseen by man,
Discreetly veiled in His eternal laws.
The sceptic sees those laws but never God.
'Why then a Deity?' he asks 'The world
Is self-sufficient in its perfectness.'
No Christian piety has ever paid
Him greater honour than that blasphemy.

(Act III, Sc. X)

The idealism which Posa expresses in such speeches as this makes him one of Schiller's most attractive figures. Yet he is more than a dreamer, he is also an intriguer for the sake of realising his ideals. He cannot resist the enjoyment of manipulating events like a God. Thus, when he has explained the plotting of Princess Eboli to the King, he refuses to take the easy way out and consult frankly with Philip on what measures should be taken. Though Posa possesses the high-mindedness of Iphigenia and stands like her as an incarnation of 'Humanity', he chooses methods that are the exact opposite of hers. For him intrigue rather than openness is the way. In order to protect Carlos from his enemies he demands of the King:

A secret
Warrant of arrest, put in my hands
By Your Royal Self, which I may instantly
Employ in danger's hour.   (Act IV, Sc. XIII)

His motive for this high-handed action, is however, insufficiently stressed in the play itself. Posa does not explain to Philip his real intentions, hinting only that fear may lead the young prince to extreme measures. Thus Philip presumably issues the warrant because he fears Carlos might rebel against him and

111

the audience are left puzzled by Posa's apparent duplicity. Has he in fact changed sides?

The careful reader of the text, and more especially of the subsequently published *Letters on Don Carlos* which devote considerable space to this point, knows better. From Letter XI, we learn that Posa's aim is to resolve his friend's fate as mysteriously

... as Providence cares for a sleep-walker—he wants to rescue him as a God would rescue him—and it is precisely this fact that dooms Carlos in the end. Both perish because Posa raises his eyes too much towards his Ideal of Virtue in the heavens and looks down too seldom towards his friend. Carlos meets his fate because his friend is not content to save him by mundane means.

Schiller supports his case in the *Letters* by apt and copious quotations from the play. There can be no doubt that he intended to paint Posa as a man whose ambitious idealism was dangerous as well as noble, and that in certain passages he has done so. Yet the structure of the play works against him. The business of Carlos's arrest by Posa emerges only as a *coup de théâtre*—the dramatist's enjoyment of the sudden twist of plot, denies the psychologist in Schiller space to express himself adequately.[1]

The same is true of two other important scenes in which Posa's enthusiasm is meant to be seen as equivocal. The first of these is the passage in which he persuades the Queen that Carlos should leave Madrid and go to command the rebel cause in the Netherlands. In Letter III Schiller tells us:

As long as Carlos remains near the Queen he is lost to the affairs of Flanders. His presence there can bring about a complete change of events. Thus Posa does not hesitate for a moment to despatch him thence in the most ruthless manner.

[1] For a careful and penetrating discussion of the literary aspects of Posa's character, see Chapter Two of E. L. Stahl's *Friedrich Schiller's Drama— Theory and Practice* (Oxford, 1954).

'   He must
Disobey the King and secretly
Set out for Brussels, where he will be greeted
With open arms. The Netherlands will rise
At his command. The righteous cause will flourish
If the King's son, himself, becomes its leader.'
Would Carlos's true friend have taken it upon himself to gamble so
recklessly with the Prince's good name and even, indeed, with his
life?

In the play, however, the Queen's reply to Posa's proposition
draws our attention away from the danger, which she mentions
only briefly, and towards the romantic panache of such an
enterprise. The audience, as opposed to the reader, has little
time to consider the ambiguity of Posa's motives when it is
immediately plunged into such lines as the following:

Queen (*after a pause*):   The plan that you propose
        Frightens me—and yet it wins my heart!
        I think you're right! It is a bold conception
        And this is why, I think, it pleases me.
        . . . .
        What you propose is great and beautiful.
        The Prince must act. How fervently I feel it!
        The role that he assumes here in Madrid
        Crushes my spirit as it must his own.
        France will be his! Savoy as well! I share
        Your own opinion, Marquis, he must act. (Act IV, Sc. III)

The psychological subtlety of Posa's character is blurred by
the surrounding speeches and action in much the same way
in a later scene of the same act. When Posa reveals to the Queen
that he has drawn suspicion on to himself and is prepared to die
that Carlos may live, Schiller intended his motives to be complex. The *Letters* make it clear that his primary intention is to
safeguard the Ideals of Freedom: Carlos, as heir to the throne,
can bring about a new regime and hence must not be allowed
to die. A secondary motive (but it *is* only secondary) is Posa's
desire to save Carlos because he is his friend. In the lines   113

spoken by Posa in the play, however, the relative importance of these two motives becomes confused. The rhetoric is dramatically effective but imprecise:

> My fortune
> Was such as few men may enjoy. I loved
> A Prince's son—in giving him my heart
> I gathered all the world into my arms.
> And I created in his single soul
> A paradise for millions. . . .
> Let him realise—
> O tell him this—that he must realise
> Our bold dream vision of a new-born State,
> Begotten by the Gods of this, our friendship.
> (Act IV, Sc. XXI)

Schiller's sense of theatre is too keen to allow Posa more precise insight into himself. Inevitably he has to speak as though his idealism and his love for Carlos are the same thing. If they were to have been separated in the way the *Letters* suggest, the play would have had to be differently constructed. It should, perhaps, have been Posa's play from the beginning and not Carlos's. But Schiller was hampered by the parts which he had already published and felt that he could not entirely abandon his original plan. Thus he is reduced to inserting hints of Posa's complexity into a total design that was not constructed to stress them. Near the end of this scene an attempt is made to allow the Queen to sum up the blind self-confidence and disregard for others which have impelled his whole intrigue:

> O, how impetuously you plunged yourself
> Into this act you call so noble! No!
> Do not deny it, for I know you now.
> How long you thirsted for it! If a thousand
> Hearts are broken, what is that to you?—
> If you can only feed your pride.   (Act IV, Sc. XXI)

But its dramatic effect is immediately lost in the remaining lines which stress only the dangers of the present situation.

More damaging to the subtlety of Posa's characterisation than anything else in the play, however, is the conventional framework in which it is set. In Act I we learn that when Carlos and Posa were boys, Carlos had taken the blame for a misdemeanour of Posa's:

Carlos: ...In shame my royal blood
          Flowed underneath the pitiless lash. I looked
          At you and did not cry. You came to me,
          Flung yourself at my feet in tears, and said
          'My pride is conquered. When you are the King
          I will repay you.'
Marquis (*giving him his hand*): I will do it, Karl.
          Now, as a man, I echo childhood's vow
          And swear I will repay....   (Act I, Sc. II)

When Posa explains to Carlos at the end of the play that he is prepared to sacrifice his life for him, he again refers to the incident:

                Listen, Karl, was I
        So quick, so willing to observe the voice
        Of conscience when, a boy, you bled for me?
                    (Act V, Sc. III)

Thus the symmetry of the story-line invites us to think of Posa's death as, in some sense, the repayment of Carlos's juvenile self-sacrifice. But, of course, the inequality of the two actions is immediately apparent: a whipping is not commensurate with death. Thus, while the power of Schiller's poetry reveals the nobility of Posa's action, the parallel suggested by the story is inept, and even though it is handled with restraint serves only to stress the motive of friendship in Posa's death at the expense of that of idealism. Letter XII explains that this desire to martyr himself as repayment for Carlos's boyhood generosity has long been in Posa's mind (as the Queen's 'How long you thirsted for it', quoted above, suggests) and should be seen as indicative of his unbalanced romanticism. Yet one feels that this is Schiller's mature self attributing motives to the character which the less-mature playwright, who designed the shape of the play, had not allowed him to express fully on the stage. That he was aware of the faults in its construction is shown by a letter to Goethe (20 March 1802):

There is a sure theatrical basis in the play and it contains much that can procure it favour. But it was, of course, not possible to make it into a satisfactory whole because it is much too broadly tailored, and I contented myself in stringing together the individual incidents so as to make the whole merely a vehicle for the separate events.

Despite its over-complicated intrigue, the idealism, theatricality and glowing verse of *Don Carlos* have ensured it a permanent place in the German theatre repertoire. It represents a watershed in Schiller's drama: on the one side lie the *Sturm und Drang* plays, on the other his great 'classical' tragedies. Before turning to these, however, we must first look at his theory of tragedy as expressed in his essays.

Schiller's Theory of Tragedy

Schiller was acutely aware that the interests of poet and dramatist may not always coincide and he discussed this problem frequently in both essays and correspondence. On 4 April 1797 he wrote to Goethe:

The more I reflect on my own craft and on the way in which the Greeks handled Tragedy, the more I find that the entire *Cardo rei* of the art lies in finding a poetic fable. The modern writer grapples painfully and anxiously with coincidence and incidentals. Because of his endeavour to come properly close to Reality, he weighs himself down with the Empty and Insignificant. By so doing he runs the risk of losing that profundity of truth in which poetry really lies. He longs to imitate an actual occurrence exactly and forgets that a poetic representation, since it is true in an absolute sense, can never coincide with reality.

The implied distinction between the modern writer and the Greek is expanded in the essay *On Naïve and Sentimental Poetry* (1797). Here Schiller stresses the fact that modern man detects a harmony in Nature which he feels lacking in himself. Nature obeys its laws unquestioningly: its very 'naturalness' contrasts with man's sense of conflict between his reason and instinct. The awareness of this conflict, since it is manifested to our feeling, Schiller terms 'Sentimental'. The Greek was unaware of this difference between himself and Nature: his attitude is, therefore, called 'Naïve'. For the Greek both Man and Nature were equally at home in the ordained pattern of the Gods:

... even their [the Greeks'] mythology was the inspiration of naïve feeling, the off-spring of a happy imagination, not that of introverted reason like the religion of later nations. Just as the Greek had not lost the naturalness of his humanity, so too he was not surprised by what he found in the natural world outside himself. ...

Modern man seeks to re-establish this sense of harmony, but his religion is of little use to him, since here too intellect is separated from emotion. As Schiller had pointed out in *The Stage Considered as a Moral Institution* (1784):

Religion no longer exists for the greater part of mankind if we take away its imagery ... and yet they are only the images of the imagination.

Beyond the dogmatics of organised religion, however, lies true religion (*i.e.* the kind indicated by Lessing's Nathan). Even an early essay like *The Stage Considered as a Moral Institution* shows Schiller proposing the theatre as a means of giving man this higher religious experience. He rejects the traditional rationalist's view of the stage as a means of inciting us to virtue by demonstrating moral behaviour. It is, he declares, the function of the Law to ensure and encourage morality, not that of the Theatre. But the laws of society are of particular, not universal, validity and in this they differ from the laws of religion. The theatre has a religious function in that its business is:

... to make vice and virtue, madness and wisdom, palpable and real to man in a thousand pictures.

Its duty, therefore, is to make us feel Vice and Virtue through lively images, not merely to hold up examples for us to follow or avoid.

The difference between Schiller's view of the stage and that of a man like Gottsched lies in the stress he puts on feeling. Yet if the theatre was to use pictures as religion did, what was it to illustrate? What were the Eternal Laws of Truth as opposed to the Temporal Laws of the State? Schiller was enabled to answer this question through his study of Kant. By doing so he established a dramatic theory and practice which exerted profound influence on both the nineteenth and twentieth centuries. Its echoes may be heard in the work of Ibsen, Tennessee Williams and Arthur Miller—to name only three. In saying this, I do not imply that such writers were consciously influenced by him (though the storm scene in *Brand* owes much to *Tell*), but rather that Schiller's writings created a climate of opinion in which it seemed possible for great tragedy to be written in the modern world. He is ultimately responsible for the stress on *choice*—Free Will—in so many subsequent plays. We detect the inheritance of Schiller's thought in the decision which has to be made by the heroine in *The Lady from the Sea*; in John Proctor's refusal to put his name to the confession of witchcraft in *The Crucible*; and in the inability of Williams's heroines to find harmony in themselves. How Schiller arrived at his theories may be seen from a brief discussion of some of his aesthetic and philosophical essays.

The Kantian distinction between Reason (*Vernunft*) and Understanding (*Verstand*) is fundamental to Schiller's thought. Understanding works entirely by the evidence of the senses: it can, for example, determine that the interior angles of any triangle add up to 180°, because the sensuous evidence of geometry has supplied it with the necessary information. The experiment may be repeated with any number of triangles and our Understanding will always supply the same answer. Once, however, we form the proposition that *all* triangles have interior angles which add up to 180°, we are passing beyond the

II

limits of Understanding. No material evidence can produce this conclusion, since it is impossible for us to draw and measure *all* possible triangles. Consequently the faculty which produces such universal conclusions is deemed by Kant to be other than Understanding and is given the name *Reason*. Since the conclusions of Reason are not based on the evidence of sense-perception, he calls them 'free', and from this, in the moral sphere, deduces his concept of Free Will.

In the moral sphere Understanding can, by weighing up the possible consequences of an action, dictate what is right or wrong in a particular case. It can, for example, determine that murder is wrong in a given circumstance. It cannot, however, evolve the Universal Commandmant 'Thou shalt not kill'. Such universal categorical imperatives can only be given by our Reason, which regards not particular circumstance but general ideas. The man who obeys the categorical imperatives of Reason is exercising his 'Free' Will—a will that is no longer dominated by the senses.

In following this line of thought, Schiller evolves in his essay *On Grace and Dignity* (1793) his concept of the Beautiful Soul:

By a beautiful soul one means that in which the moral feeling of all human sensibilities has finally become so secure that it may uninhibitedly leave the conduct of the will to the emotions, without running the risk of their being contrary to the decisions of the will.

Thus the Beautiful Soul is one whose spirit is so far consonant with the imperatives of Reason that it instinctively acts morally. The lack of conflict in such a person gives rise to Grace, which Schiller further defines as 'Beauty of movement'. True Grace is the sign of inner harmony and in this connection he warns actresses against the adoption of 'false Grace':

Out of the smile of true Grace is made the most repulsive grimace; the lovely play of the eyes, so enchanting when true sensibility speaks from them, becomes a distortion; the melting, modulating voice, so irresistible in a true mouth, becomes a studied tremulo and

119

the whole music of female charm turns to a deceptive artificiality of appearance.

Once, however, the Beautiful Soul is faced with an emotional crisis (as, of course, it must be in Tragedy), it evolves into what Schiller calls the Sublime Soul. In this case, Reason

. . . which has brought the inclinations to its allegiance and merely consigned guidance to the senses, will, in the very moment that baser instinct seeks to misuse its power, withdraw that guidance from it . . . the Beautiful Soul will become heroic and raise itself to pure intelligence.

Here, then, a new harmony is created: the Sublime Soul is not instinctively virtuous (as is the Beautiful Soul), it passes through a crisis and eventually freely and willingly accepts the dictates of Reason.

The distinction between Beauty and Sublimity for Schiller lies in the fact that Sublimity implies a struggle which is eventually resolved, whereas Beauty immediately soothes and satisfies. In *On the Sublime* (1793–1800) he writes:

If it were not for the Sublime, Beauty would make us forget our Dignity as human-beings.

That is to say that Beauty offers no challenge to our Reason. The Dignity of which he speaks here, he explains in *On Grace and Dignity* as 'the outward manifestation' of 'the control of the instincts by spiritual power'. Since Beauty appeals instantly to both senses and intellect, it fails to remind us that we have this power. But the 'mixed feeling' of fear and delight which we find in contemplating a wild mountain landscape such as Ossian describes, immediately makes us aware of disharmony in ourselves. It makes us aware, in other words, of our true nature. Such a landscape strikes us as being more than Beautiful —it is Sublime. Its very challenge reminds us of the dictum of Nathan (quoted by Schiller at the beginning of his essay) 'No man is compelled to be compelled'.

It was this Sublime Freedom of man which Schiller sought to demonstrate in his tragedies. In the essay *On the Pathetic* (1793) he again stresses his earlier point that the function of Tragedy is to move us to sympathy rather than to give us moral example:

...the tragic hero must first of all establish himself as a being capable of feeling before we will honour him as one capable of Reason and believe in his strength of soul.

It is because the hero suffers that we sympathise with him and yet, we are warned:

The representation of suffering—as mere suffering—is never the end of art, although as a means to that end it is of the greatest importance.

Suffering, then, is only depicted as a means of demonstrating the hero's subsequent Sublimity. That Sublimity may be shown in two ways: either Actively or Passively.

Passive Sublimity Schiller understands as a state of mind in which the hero rises superior to his suffering. As an example of it he cites Milton's Satan greeting the horrors of damnation with Stoic courage. By Active Sublimity he understands a condition in which the hero's suffering is brought about by his own volition. Either he chooses to follow a moral course which must entail suffering, or (an alternative form of Active Sublimity) he inwardly repents the evil of some past dead.

It was the form of Active Sublimity involving repentance, which Schiller saw as particularly pertinent to Tragedy, since it stressed moral potential rather than moral achievement. The spectacle of a brave man choosing good and suffering for its sake is morally edifying, but the sight of a man who repents is more moving and aesthetically satisfying. It depicts not merely the admirable achievement of one particular human being, but stresses the moral capacity which is common to all men. To stress this is the final aim of tragic art, as Schiller reveals in *On the Sublime* where he re-defines Aristotle's theory of Purgation in terms of Kantian philosophy:

The Pathetic is an artificial misfortune and like actual misfortune places us in immediate contact with the spiritual law that rules in our breasts. Actual misfortune, however, does not always choose well either its man or its time. It often surprises us without defences and, what is worse, it renders us defenceless. The artificial misfortune of the Pathetic, however, discovers us fully armed and, since it is merely fictitious, affords the independent principle in our minds room to establish its absolute freedom. The more often the spirit renews this kind of independence, the better advantage it gains over the baser instincts, so that finally, when imaginary and artificial misfortune is replaced by actual misfortune, the spirit is able to deal with the actual misfortune as though it were imaginary and—highest reach of human nature!—resolve actual suffering into a sublime emotion. Thus one can say that the Pathetic is an innoculation of unavoidable fate whereby its evil is removed from it and its attack directed to the stronger side of man.

For Aristotle's 'Purgation', then, we have Schiller's 'innoculation of unavoidable fate'. The theatre innoculates against misfortune by giving us a calculated, artificial dose and by reminding us that man's freedom is his noblest characteristic.

Throughout his essays Schiller insists that Tragedy must stress action, though by this he means spiritual action rather than outward and visible stage business. Ideally, he held, the visible action should reflect the inward:

Two things are the concern of the poet and artist: that he should raise himself above reality and that he should remain standing within the sensuous. Where these two things are united there is aesthetic art.   (Letter to Goethe, 14 September 1797)

That the uniting of the aspects was not always easy to him, however, is shown by the letter already quoted at the beginning of this section (4 April 1797). He touches on the same difficulty in the essay on *The Use of the Chorus in Tragedy*, which is prefaced to *The Bride of Messina*:

... reflective thought must also have its place in Tragedy. If it is to deserve this place, however, it must regain by means of expository speech what it finds lacking in sensuous life.

Words, then, must be allowed to speak louder than actions. The length of many of the speeches in Schiller's plays (which, as a letter to Goethe of 24 August 1798 reveals, gave even the author some misgivings) is partially attributable to this. Yet more laconic speech, he argued, would have been too realistic and particular.

Having stressed the need for expository speech in Tragedy, the essay on *Use of the Chorus* continues:

... when the two elements of poetry, the Ideal and the Sensuous, do not work together by virtue of inner unity, they must work side by side—or else poetry is annulled. If the balance is not perfectly attained from within then equipoise can only be achieved by adjusting the two scales.

In other words the dramatist must make conscious adjustments: a drama, in Schiller's view, need not always be an imaginative unity, but rather a controlled pattern of parallels where poetry and stage action run 'side by side'. This attitude is borne out by his method of writing: he composed his plays, or at least whole sections of them, as literary compositions in the first place. Only subsequently did he undertake the tasks of cutting and re-writing for the theatre—a task which he confessed to Goethe on 22 December 1798 to be 'astonishingly painful and time-destroying'. Although there is ample evidence in the plays themselves that he had a sure sense of, and delight in, the theatrical, the philosopher-poet in Schiller had something of a disdain for the tasks of the dramatist-director:

The fashioning of the play [*Wallenstein*] for the theatre, as a mere business of the Understanding, I can easily undertake alongside another peculiarly theoretical task.

(Letter to Goethe, 31 August 1798)

On 5 January of the same year he had confessed to Goethe his inability to invent suitable dramatic fables for himself. The need for the poet to 'raise himself above reality' seemed to postulate that reality should be given to him by history:

123

I will allow myself to be denied the choice of all subject-matter save the historical. Freely invented material would be my rock. To idealise what is realistic is quite a different operation from realising the Ideal, and this last is the real case with free fiction. I am capable of bringing to life conditioned, given and confined material, of giving it warmth and releasing the sources within it at the same time. Also the objective definity of such stuff bridles my imagination and resists my arbitrary fancy.

From *Don Carlos* onward, he was faithful to historical subjects with the single and notable exception of *The Bride of Messina*. Not, of course, that any of his plays are strictly true to historical fact. Schiller always invented freely, following Aristotle in his belief that poetry had a different function from that of history:

Tragedy has a poetic aim, that is to say it represents an action in order to move us and, by so doing, to entertain us. Provided, therefore, it treats the given material consistently with this aim, it is accordingly free in its mode of Imitation: it is granted power, indeed it is obliged, to submit the historical truth to the laws of poetry and to fashion the given material according to the laws of art.

(On Tragic Art, 1792)

Wallenstein

The writing of the Wallenstein trilogy (*Wallenstein's Camp, The Piccolomini* and *Wallenstein's Death*) occupied Schiller from 1791–9 and is one of his major achievements. Its strongest appeal, however, is inevitably to a German audience rather than an international one, if only because the name Wallenstein invokes an immediate response in the German mind, as say, Cromwell or Elizabeth I does in the British. In writing the plays Schiller made considerable dramatic use of this fact. Wallenstein, himself, does not appear in the *Camp* and his appearances in *The Piccolomini* are few. He is, however, constantly referred to and his presence haunts the plays as much as Julius Caesar's does Shakespeare's tragedy.

Against this sombre scene of time is painted
An enterprise of daring arrogance:
A character of rash audacity.
You know him well—creator of great armies,
The idol of his camp, the scourge of lands,
The Emperor's crutch and then the Emperor's terror,
Fortune's adventurous son, who, borne aloft
By favour of the time, was quickly raised
To honour's highest pinnacle; yet still
Unsatisfied, strove higher, till he fell
The victim of unbridled lust for power.

(Prologue to Wallenstein's Camp)

Julius Caesar was much in Schiller's mind when he wrote the trilogy and many speeches instantly recall Shakespeare's text:

Illo: O use this hour before it slips away!
    The moment of true import and success
    So seldom comes in life. Decision waits
    On chance encounters, happy accidents;
    And only here and there can we perceive
    The stems of Fortune—opportunities
    Which under pressure from some point of time
    Put forth their buds. Look round you and consider
    With what decision, what portentous fate,
    The heads of all the armies gather here:
    The best and finest men who only wait
    The slightest signal from your king-like hand.
    Then do not let them leave! In this whole war
    You'll never find them brought together thus.
    It is the swelling tide that lifts the weight
    Of vessels from the shore—and every spirit
    Is raised by currents that control the crowd.
    Now they are here! You have them now! But soon
    The war will sunder them. The common cause
    Will be consumed by petty interests
    And private cares. Whereas today the tide
    May bear a man till he forgets himself,
    He'll wake more soberly and feel his weakness.
. . . .

> You always wait the stars' appointed hour
> So long, you loose the earthly one! Believe me
> The stars of destiny are in your breast.
> Your Venus is decision, self-reliance.[2]
>
>   (*The Piccolomini*, Act II, Sc. VI)

Yet although the imagery is full of Shakespearean overtones, the voice is unmistakably Schiller's own. The movement of the lines is more leisurely than Shakespeare's, images are expanded more fully and there is more of the sense of an operatic aria. At the same time the language is vigorous and rhetorically suited to the stage. The frenetic outbursts of *Sturm und Drang* dialogue have been bridled and controlled by the poet's experience of pentameters in *Don Carlos* and in the course of writing *Wallenstein* he made an important discovery about the nature of dramatic verse:

> In the course of my present work I have noticed something which you, perhaps, have already discovered. It seems that a part of the poetic interest lies in the antagonism between content and representation: if the content is full of poetic significance it is well-suited by a plain representation and a simplicity of expression which touches on the commonplace. On the other hand where the content is unpoetic and commonplace, as in general must be the case so often, it is given poetic dignity through lively and rich expression. This is also the occasion, in my opinion, where the Decoration which Aristotle demands must come in—for in a poetic work nothing should be commonplace.   (Letter to Goethe, 24 November 1797)

There are moments in *Wallenstein* where Schiller achieves great poetry by the simplest means—when he writes the kind of verse which has allowed his poetry to become part of modern German speech, so that he is quoted unconsciously by his countrymen as Shakespeare is with us. He combines the quality of natural conversation with poetic profundity. An example is found in Wallenstein's last lines where the dramatic irony of his simple

---

[2] Cf. *Julius Caesar* Act. IV, Sc. III (Brutus's 'There is a tide in the affairs of men') and Act I, Sc. II (Cassius's 'The fault, dear Brutus, is not in our stars/But in ourselves . . . ').

statements achieves poignance and dignity. In Act V, Sc. II, Buttler and Deveroux decide his ambition can only be halted by his death:

Deveroux: Is it his aim, then, to dethrone the Emperor?
Buttler: It is! To rob him of his throne and life.
Deveroux: And if we should deliver him alive
          To Vienna, he would perish on the scaffold?
Buttler: That stroke of fate is one he *can't* avoid.
Deveroux: Macdonald, come! He'll end his days a general—
          And fall with honour at his soldiers' hands.

(Wallenstein's Death)

Wallenstein's fate is sealed. Even though the troops who rebel against him are sensitive to his dignity and magic as a commander of men, there is no escape from the final act of murder. It is against this knowledge and Wallenstein's own ignorance of the plot that we set his last words to Gordon:

> If you think
> My fortune has deserted me, then leave.
> Take off my clothes for this last time and go,
> Forsake my ranks and join your Emperor.
> Goodnight, Gordon!
> I think that I shall sleep ... and sleep ... tonight.
> The labour of the last few days was great.
> See that they do not waken me too early.

(Ibid., Act V, Sc. V)

It is the sheer simplicity of the words that make them so moving.

Paradoxically, part of Schiller's success in *Wallenstein* is, perhaps, attributable to the fact that he found his hero unsympathetic. On 28 November 1796, he wrote to Goethe:

I could almost say that the subject does not interest me at all and I have never united in myself such coldness for my subject with such warmth for my work.

From this grew an objectivity towards his hero, whose character he also examined as a historian in his *History of the Thirty Years*   127

War. In the play there is no suggestion that Wallenstein becomes a Sublime Soul, as do Mary Stuart and St. Joan in
Schiller's hands. Here there is only the sense of ambition which
leads to nothingness. From the devotion of Max Piccolomini
and the respect paid to him even by those who rebel against
him, we learn to honour Wallenstein. In his ambition there is
something majestic, in his Hamlet-like indecision something
moving. But in the end there is only quiet dignity left—not even
the same defiance of misfortune which Satan exhibits in hell.
The compass of his tragedy—his rebellion against the Emperor
and ambition to make himself a king; his refusal, from political
motives, to allow his daughter, Thekla, to marry Max; his loss
of Max, himself, his 'dearest friend'—is compressed into the
earlier lines of his speech to Gordon:

> Never can
> The Emperor forgive me. Could he do so,
> I could not let myself accept forgiveness.
> If I had known before, what now is past—
> That it would cost my dearest friend his life—
> And if my heart had spoken as it speaks
> Today, it may be I'd have thought . . . may be . . .
> And may be not. What shall we seek to save?
> This cannot end in nothing when the start
> Was quickened by such lofty purposes.
> So let it run its course! (*Going to the window.*)
> The night has come already! Look, the castle
> Lies in stillness. Lights, there, bring some light!
> (*Ibid.*, Act V, Sc. V.)

Despite the last lingering hope of Wallenstein's superstition—
that what has begun so well cannot end in nothing—his
catastrophe is unavoidable.

There is much in his situation that suggests that of Caesar,
even including the fact that both believe in predestination and
heed the warnings of astrologers. The figure of Wallenstein,
however, is differently placed in the scheme of the drama from
that of Shakespeare's dictator. Caesar appears at the beginning

of the play, is murdered in Act III and reappears as a ghost in Act IV. Not only is his physical presence (as distinct from references to him) evenly distributed throughout the work, whereas Wallenstein's as we have seen is not, the dramatic interest is not finally focused on his personal tragedy. Schiller chose to make Wallenstein his hero, yet only allowed him to be dramatically dominant in the last of the three plays. *The Camp* merely sets the scene: it has no story but relies on lively representation of the background with a cast of more than thirty characters, none of whom have principle roles in the other two plays. *The Piccolomini* is basically concerned with Lieutenant-General Octavio Piccolomini and his son, Max. Octavio, partly out of loyalty to the Emperor and partly from a desire to feather his own nest, plots against Wallenstein and hence Max is faced with a typically Schillerian choice: either loyalty to the Emperor or loyalty to Wallenstein, his friend. Eventually he chooses the path of duty, loyalty to the Emperor, and it is his inward conflict that dominates the play. Thus *Wallenstein's Death*, with its concentration on Wallenstein himself, is only loosely connected to the dramatic scheme of its predecessors, though tightly bound to their political and historical theme. For this reason it is not entirely satisfactory when, as sometimes happens in the modern German theatre, *Wallenstein's Death* is performed as a single play. It requires the other two pieces to give it full significance, even though the trilogy as a whole lacks dramatic unity.

The fragmentary nature of its total construction is stressed by the way the plays were first presented at Weimar. The short play, *Wallenstein's Camp* was presented for the opening of the new theatre on 12 October 1798. (Kotzebue's *The Corsican* completed the evening.) When *The Piccolomini* followed on 30 January 1799, the first four acts were compressed into two, the the fifth act of the printed version became the third, and the fourth and fifth acts were made up of the first two acts of *Wallenstein's Death*. When the *Death* was performed on 20 April 1799, its remaining three acts were divided up into the statutory

five. Such divisions certainly savour of the work of Understanding, rather than that of imaginative insight and poetic
idealism.

The production of the *Camp* was undertaken by Goethe. He
made careful study of wood-cuts of camp life during the Thirty
Years War and saw that costumes had a historical veracity
which, at the same time, did not conflict with his notions of
beauty. He also held it important that any costume should
indicate a universal type rather than an idiosyncratic individual. His attention to details is illustrated by a letter to Schiller
on the day of the first performance of *The Piccolomini*:

1. Will you not have Vohs [Max Piccolomini] enter in a cuirass in
   the first scene? He looks far too sober in his jerkin.
2. Nor should we forget the cap for Wallenstein—there must be
   something in the nature of heron's feathers somewhere in the
   wardrobe.
3. Wouldn't you give Wallenstein another red cloak? It looks so
   very much like the other one from the back.

Both poets were aware that the production would tax the
resources of the company to the full and roles had to be doubled
and even trebled. But throughout the preparation of the scripts
for the theatre, Schiller was true to his promise to Goethe (18
September 1798) 'to keep our Weimar personnel always in my
eye'. Accordingly he wrote the part of 'Peter Longshanks' (*der
lange Peter*) in the *Camp* to suit the physical characteristics of the
actor, August Leissring, and introduced Thekla's songs to
demonstrate the vocal talents of Karoline Jagemann. Great
attention in the *Camp* was paid to movement and bustling life.
Actors were allowed considerable freedom, and careful grouping, in front of a painted backcloth of tents and trees, conveyed
the requisite impression with the minimum of performers.

In directing *The Piccolomini*, Goethe strove to make Max the
central figure. Here Schiller's interest as a lyrical poet really
lay and in Max the moral issue is made most clear. His scene
with Wallenstein in Act II of *The Death* (Act V of *The Piccolo-*

mini on the Weimar stage) strongly portrays his conflict between
friendship and duty:

Max (*with emphasis*): O fear these agencies of falsehood! Fear them!
    They will not hold their word, these lying wraiths
    That beckoning lure you to the deep abyss.
    I warn you, do not trust them—but turn back
    To duty. You are given power to do it!
    Send me to Vienna. *I* will do it.
    I'll make your peace there with the Emperor.
    He does not know you, I know you so well,
    And he shall see you with my eye of Truth
    And I bring back his confidence in you.
                    (*Wallenstein's Death*, Act II, Sc. II)

In thus stressing the figure of Max in the production and insist-
ing throughout on careful speaking of the verse, Goethe did
Schiller great service. He was able, indeed, on 5 October 1798,
to report:

Leissring, Weyrauch and Haide speak the rhymed verse [used in the
Camp] as though they had never spoken anything else all the days
of their lives. Haide, in particular, speaks the end of a period as I
have never heard it done in the German theatre.

In handling the supernatural elements of the plays, Wallenstein's belief in astrology, Goethe was less helpful. Schiller had
doubts on the subject and hoped to use his hero's superstition to
emphasise his conflict with fate and circumstance. Goethe, on
the other hand, had no such doubts. He argued that since
astronomers could demonstrate the disturbance of one group of
stars by another, it was clear that the world itself was subject
to the laws of the solar system. Belief in superstitious astrology,
therefore, could be seen as a manifestation of man's dark
feeling of unity with the whole of creation. Had Schiller contented himself with treating the subject in this way, all might
have been well. But the temptation to use omens and prog-
nostications for sheer dramatic effect proved too strong for

him. As Coleridge pointed out,[3] the plays contain a basic contradiction in this respect: on the one hand Schiller mocks the superstition, on the other he uses it as though it were true.

Mary Stuart

In the essay *On Tragic Art* Schiller writes:

It is invariably injurious to the highest perfection of his work when the poet cannot dispense with a villain and is compelled to show depth of malice as the cause of depth of suffering.

The same thought may have been in his mind when writing Act I of *Mary Stuart*. Here it is made clear that Mary deceives herself when she agrees with Mortimer that her right to the English throne is

> The only cause of all my suffering. (Act I, Sc. VI)

Elizabeth is not her only enemy, there is also Mary's own past. It is the revelation of this past in the scene with Hanna Kennedy that makes Mary a complex and arresting figure as well as a pathetic one:

Mary: It is the blood-drenched shadow of King Darnley,
Rising in anger from his hollow vault!
And he will never make his peace with me
Until my depth of suffering is filled.
Hanna: What thoughts are these—?
Mary: You have forgotten, Hanna.
My memory is not so weak. Today
The dreadful anniversary of his death
Returns. I keep it, penitent and fasting.
. . . .
Hanna: You did not kill him! Others did that deed.
Mary: I knew of it. I let them act. I lured him
By my caresses to the net of death.   (Act I, Sc. IV)

[3] See Coleridge's Translation of *The Piccolomini* and *Wallenstein's Death*.

In vain Hanna tries to console her mistress, pointing out that Darnley had ordered Rizzio to be killed before Mary's eyes and that, therefore, she had done no more than take 'blood revenge for shedding blood'. Mary, however, replies:

> That blood
> Will seek my own in vengeance for itself.
> You try to comfort me—you speak my sentence.

The precise details of Mary's guilt are left vague. 'I knew of it. I let them act.' From this and her other statements it is impossible to decide the real nature of her guilt. In this respect she resembles Harry in T. S. Eliot's *The Family Reunion*, for in both plays stress is laid on guilt rather than crime: the particular circumstances are undefined in order to draw attention to the universal emotion.

Throughout the play the image of blood-guilt pursues Mary. Elizabeth, for example, untruthfully reminds her:

> That you have sought to compass my own death.
>
> (Act III, Sc. IV)

And in the same scene declares:

> No man is now ambitious to become
> Your *fourth* husband, for you kill your suitors
> As you do your husbands.

Mortimer, Mary's passionate admirer, is willing for her sake to kill not only Elizabeth but his own uncle and all who stand in Mary's path. Yet the sense of guilt incurred by Darnley's death is so strong in her that she steadfastly rejects murder as a means of furthering her cause:

> All that the laws of chivalry and right
> Permit in war may be my lawful means,
> But both my pride and conscience must reject
> The secret act of bloodshed. Murder would
> Stain both my hand and honour. I say honour!
>
> (Act I, Sc. VII)

133

From the beginning of the play she has pleaded for a Catholic priest to whom she may make confession of her guilt. Historically speaking this was denied her, but Schiller, as we have seen, held that a poet in his search for universal truth need not be bound by history. Accordingly in the last act he invents the fact that Melvil, Mary's steward, has been secretly ordained: he is thus able to grant her absolution and give her Holy Communion. This scene, though Goethe found Communion on the stage distasteful and cautioned Schiller against representing it, must be counted one of the dramatist's most imaginative departures from historical fact. The implausibility of Melvil's being ordained for the specific purpose of his visit to Mary in prison, is certainly outbalanced by the naturalistic means it affords the heroine of baring her soul. Since it was Schiller's intention to exhibit Mary in a state of Active Sublimity, and since that Sublimity lies in moral potential rather than moral action, what better way to present it on the stage than in the confessional? Where could one find closer unity between physical image and poetic significance? Yet Schiller does not stop at confession and repentance. The unity of stage action and poetic image is pushed to its extreme when Melvil allows Mary (contrary to the usage of the Roman Church) to receive the Blood of Christ as well as the Body.

> Melvil: Receive the Blood which has been shed for you—
> You may receive, by Papal dispensation.
> The Holy Father grants to you in death
> The highest right of kings, the priesthood's due.

A moment before, in granting her absolution, Melvile has said:

> Blood expiates the guilt of blood's transgression.
> (Act V, Sc. VII)

Thus the Blood of Christ becomes the outward and visible symbol of Mary's freedom from the guilt of Darnley's blood. She has at last succeeded in doing what Hanna urged on her in Act I—she has made peace with herself. By accepting her execution as the means of demonstrating her true penitence, she acquires Freedom, not only from Elizabeth, whose charges against her are unjust, but from her own inner torment.

Elizabeth never achieves Freedom in this way. Where Mary finally accepts the Categorical Imperative of Reason, Elizabeth remains throughout a creature of Understanding. It is inevitably Understanding rather than Reason that dictates the temporal laws of political life and the point is implicit in Schiller's distinction, already mentioned, between religion and law in *On Dramatic Art*. Elizabeth is always the politician, the slave of circumstance and expediency. She is well aware of her slavery and significantly seeks to avoid further chains—especially, for example, the chain of marriage with France. Drawing her ring from her finger, she gives it to the French Ambassador with the words:

> Give His Highness, then, this gift. It is
> Not yet a link within a chain to bind me,
> But bondage may be born of such a ring.
> (Act II, Sc. II)

She can gain no Freedom, for she thinks only of immediate advantage. In the end she shares something of Wallenstein's disillusionment—weary not only of life but the very business of political decisions:

> O, Shrewsbury, you saved my life today,
> Deflecting murder's dagger from my flesh.
> Why did you not allow it what it would?
> All quarrels would be ended then, all doubts
> Sundered from me. Freed from guilt, I'd lie
> Within the stillness of my vault. O, God,
> I am weary of life and weary, too, of ruling.
> (Act IV, Sc. IX)

To the last Elizabeth tries in vain to shake off the shackles her own judgements make for her. Her eventual reasons for signing Mary's death-warrant betray her desire for freedom, yet she seeks it in the wrong way. Up to this point she has spared

135

K

Mary, though she realises she has done so for reasons of political necessity only:

> But was it, then, my own free choice that led me
> To act impartially? Omnipotent
> Necessity, that even curbs the will
> And choice of Kings, dictated me that virtue.
>
> (Act IV, Sc. X)

In the moment of test the political dictates of Understanding cannot keep her baser instincts, her womanly jealousy, in check:

> Her head shall fall, then! I will have my freedom
> . . . .
> . . . . She took my lover from me,
> Robbed me of my bridegroom. Mary Stuart
> Is written large on every circumstance
> Of my defeated fortune. If she lives
> No longer, I am free as mountain air.   (*Ibid.*)

Yet she shuns even the responsibility for the warrant she has signed:

> Davison (*in terror, looking at the paper*): Your Majesty! Your name? You have decided?
> Elizabeth: I have signed that warrant.
> That much was asked of me. A piece of paper
> Makes no decision and a signature,
> A name, has not the power to kill.   (Act IV, Sc. XI)

Davison is left in doubt of her intention, it is Burleigh who seizes the warrant from him and sees that it is carried out. Elizabeth's perfidious cruelty in sending Davison to the Tower robs her even of our pity. She is not a tragic figure (as some English productions seem to suggest), but neither is she the mere villainess which some critics have held her to be. Vindictive and unprincipled, she is still human. Indeed her humanity is more easily recognisable than Mary's in the last act of the play. There is something superhuman in Mary's eventual Sublimity, and it was, perhaps, because he sensed this that Schiller decided to end the play with Elizabeth's loneliness rather than Mary's death. The final scene returns us, as it were, to earth after Mary's glimpse of heaven: by recalling the actual circumstances of human existence it stresses the reality of Mary's vision of the Ideal. Without the final scenes at Elizabeth's Court the last words of Mary ('Fare well!—I now have nothing left on earth') might seem too remote and idealistic. By returning us to Elizabeth, Schiller keeps touch with the Sensuous at the same time as directing our attention to the Ideal.

The co-existence of the Sensuous and Ideal is demonstrated in *Mary Stuart* more constantly than in any other play by Schiller. It is most clearly demonstrated in the third act where the two queens confront each other. Their meeting is unhistorical, but since history shows the two in political opposition it is entirely natural for a dramatic representation of history to present them in physical confrontation. The stage image portrays the historical implication, enriching it with Schiller's psychological and philosophical insight. The same coincidence of action, character, poetry and philosophy is found in such a speech as Mortimer's description of his visit to Italy in Act I, Sc. VI. When Mortimer describes his conversion to the Roman Church he speaks both as a man of the sixteenth century, fascinated by the imagery of Catholicism, and also as a typical child of Weimar, fascinated by the beauty of Italian Classicism. It is significant that he mentions first the Colosseum and then the beauty of Christian churches. The spirit of Goethe's *Italian Journey* is married to the situation of Mary Stuart's admirer. Nor is there any sense of conflict between the two: the poetry arises from instinctive unity not from intellectual parallelism:

> Imagine it, Your Majesty!
> The great triumphal arches rose before me,
> The Colosseum's splendour circumscribed
> My wondering gaze. Olympian spirit ringed
> My soul with sculptured miracles of brightness!

137

I'd never felt the power of art before—
The Church that reared me shunned all sensuous joy,
All images of beauty, honoured only
The incorporeal word. Imagine it!
I walked in churches where the songs of heaven
Poured forth their diapason, where profusion
Of painted figures burnished walls and vault.
The holiest and highest palpable
To my delighted sense. I saw them all:
The Angel's greeting and Our Lord's own birth,
His Holy Mother, and the Trinity
Descending. Christ's Transfiguration—saw
The Pope in radiance saying Mass and blessing
The faithful.
                What is gold? What glittering jewels
That deck the majesty of earthly kings?
He, only, wears the halo of God's light,
His house alone is heaven's kingdom here:
These forms were not created in this world.

                               (Act I, Sc. VI)

Mortimer, like Posa, is a dreamer whose enthusiasm is dangerous to those he loves. Like Posa, he sacrifices himself. As he does so he sets a conscious example to Mary:

O, my beloved, since I could not save you,
I give you, as a man, a man's example.

                               (Act IV, Sc. IV)

Betrayed by the treachery of Leicester, he stabs himself, claiming Freedom as he does so:

In this last moment I will free my heart
And loose my tongue in freedom.   *(Ibid.)*

The contrast between Mortimer and Leicester at the end of the play echoes that between Mary and Elizabeth. Mortimer dies cursing those who have been unfaithful to the 'earthly Mary' as they have to the 'heavenly One', and his last words stress his devotion to the Ideal:

> Holy Mary pray for me
> And take me to you in Eternal Life.   (*Ibid.*)

Leicester, on the other hand, who has attempted to gain the favour of both queens and played the politician's game throughout, realises the essential contrast between Mary and himself as she moves towards the scaffold:

> —She goes, a soul transfigured! And I stay
> Doomed to despair forever with the damned.
>
> (Act V, Sc. X)

Though *Mary Stuart* is Schiller's greatest play, its first performance in Weimar (14 June 1800) disappointed him in some respects. He had intended the role of Mary for Karoline Jagemann, but in the event it was played by Madame Vohs— her first great tragic part. Jagemann played Elizabeth and scored a great success, but Vohs stressed the suffering of Mary too greatly and in the confrontation scene was too lacrimose and complaining. At the end of the act it seemed that Elizabeth, not Mary, had won the battle. What Vohs apparently missed was the potential strength of the character. In her defence, it must be said that many of Mary's lines inevitably express her complaints, and the confinement of the action to the period between her judgement and execution brings much reporting of past events. It is, therefore, essential for an actress to study the implication of her words in the context of the whole work, rather than that of the individual speech. Thus, Mary's request for a Catholic priest in Act I must show not only her deprivation but also her sense of right—though the immediate text, itself, may not suggest this:

> Here in my prison, I've been long denied
> The Church's consolation: sacraments.
> She who has robbed me of my throne and freedom
> And threatens my own life, will not desire
> To close the very doors of heaven to me.   (Act I, Sc. II)

When Mortimer declares his physical passion for her (Act III,   139

Sc. VI), reminding her that she gave herself to Rizzio and Bothwell, her reactions (conveyed in the text by the words 'Leave me! Have your senses left you?') must convey not only her immediate fear but also her sense of guilt, since we know from her conversations with Hanna that there is wounding truth in Mortimer's words. The text, then, like that of Shakespeare and Chekhov gathers richness as it unrolls. It was, therefore, not altogether surprising that the inexperienced Madame Vohs was outshone by Jagemann who had in Elizabeth the easier and more explicit role.

The Maid of Orleans

Schiller's next drama portrayed not a sinner who became a near-saint, but a saint whom he chose to show as a near-sinner. His method with Joan of Arc was to stress the divine in her from the start—we never, in fact, see her as a simple peasant, for the Prologue, in which her father, Thibaut, marries off her two sisters, culminates in Joan's statement of her heavenly mission:

> For He, who spoke to Moses on Mount Horeb
> . . . .
> Spoke here to me as springtime leaves unfurled:
> 'Go forth! And be my witness to the world.
> Roughness of metal shall encase your limb,
> Ungentle steel be armoured round your breast.
> No love for mortal man may ever win
> Your heart with shameful fire of passion's quest.
> Your head shall bear no bridal-crown's soft rim,
> No loving infant flourish at your breast!
> But radiant, honoured in the battle's fame
> All women shall do homage to your name.'
>
> (Prologue, Sc. IV)

The use of rhymed verse for this soliloquy is dramatically significant, since it contrasts with the blank verse of the earlier scenes and calls attention to the unworldliness of Joan's mission.

A similar device is used in Act II, Sc. VII, where Joan encounters Montgomery and warns him that God will punish the English for invading France. Here the lines turn from pentameters to hexameters and this form is significantly carried through to Joan's prayer in the next scene:

> Virgin sublime, you work your fearful powers through me!
> You gird with strength this arm, unpractised in war's art,
> You, only, case my heart with total lack of pity.
>
> (Act II, Sc. VIII)

This attempt to portray Joan as superhuman has, however, the effect of making her, at the same time, inhuman. The amazonian in her triumphs over the saintly in such moments as that in which she tells Montgomery:

> For it is fatal to encounter me,
> The Maid, who is bound by vow inflexible to serve
> The invincible kingdom of heaven, to slay all living men
> The God of battle sends so fatefully against her.
>
> (Act II, Sc. VII)

Her bombastic greeting to him at the start of the scene is a further example of this:

> Your death is near! The womb that gave you life was British.

The patriotic element in the play has been attributed by some critics to Schiller's desire to awaken unity among the German-speaking peoples against the threat of Napoleon. Against this, however, others have argued with more plausibility, that if the intention were primarily anti-French propaganda, the choice of St. Joan as a heroine is extraordinary. While it is true, as Professor Bruford points out,[4] that both this play and *Wilhelm Tell* played an important part in the recovery of German morale after the defeat of the Prussians by Napoleon at Jena in 1806, and also helped 'in the preparation of the War

---

[4] See W. H. Bruford, *Theatre, Drama and Audience in Goethe's Germany* (Routledge & Kegan Paul, London, 1950), p. 331.

of Liberation', it was not Schiller's intention, here or elsewhere, to confine his drama to particular issues. When Joan asks:

> For what is innocent, holy, human good,
> If not the struggle for our fatherland?
>
> (Act II, Sc. X)

—patriotism is represented as the occasion for Sublime action rather than an immediate call to arms. Schiller was more concerned with the morals of his countrymen than their political struggle with France and, as Stahl observes, we find scarcely any reference to the Revolutionary wars in his correspondence 'and nowhere do we find him expressing sentiments that may be called nationalistic'.[5]

Certainly some passages in *The Maid* show an attitude to the 'glories' of war which is no longer acceptable, but then so do the historical plays of Shakespeare. It is, on the whole, much easier to make allowance for such passages than it is for Schiller's treatment of supernatural elements in the play. While war forms the background to Joan's conflict, her relationship to God is of its essence. Her vow of virginity stands, in Schillerian terms, for her duty to follow the Categorical Imperative of morality. What, however, we ask ourselves, has Reason to do with second sight, or with the working of miracles that seem to defy Reason's laws? Why is Joan able to perceive the exact details of the Dauphin's secret prayers (Act I, Sc. X) and to break the heavy chains binding her arms and body at the end of the play? Whereas Shaw presents the miracles as either natural occurrences (the changing of the wind on the Loire), or simple events exaggerated by superstitious ignorance (the laying of the hens in Scene I and Joan's reported escape from the tower), Schiller exploits the miraculous theatrically, ignoring its implied contradiction of his philosophical premises. The conflict of the supernatural and the rational, already noted in *Wallenstein*, is therefore repeated in this play with even more damaging results.

142   [5] Stahl, *op. cit.*, p. 117.

The unity of the Sensuous and the Ideal, complete in *Mary Stuart*, is only partial in *The Maid*. Again Schiller departs from history, but on this occasion with less imaginative justification. History afforded no hint of a moral crisis in Joan. True, she was burned at the stake, but as Shaw pointed out, sainthood is something more than being burned alive. Schiller's desire to demonstrate Joan's moral potential inevitably led him to depict a death for which she, herself, might seem more immediately responsible: accordingly she escapes from prison, wins the day for France and dies on the battlefield. Before this, however, we witness her moral conflict, temptation and regeneration. Towards the end of the third act Joan begins to be presented in a new light. Hitherto she has been the incarnation of heavenly power; thereafter she becomes a human being who finds it difficult to reconcile humanity with her mission. The crux of the play is the scene in which she meets Lionel, the English leader. It is prepared for by the encounter with the Black Knight (Act III, Sc. IX), a supernatural figure who reveals the doubt encroaching on her soul. The Black Knight warns her to:

> Forsake
> This fortune which has served you like a slave
> Before its anger seeks to free itself:
> It is perfidious, serves none to the end.

In a letter to Goethe (16 September 1803), Schiller observed that the Knight's lines might be delivered with a certain monotony and that little movement was called for in the part— he is clearly designed as the voice of Joan's fear. In the next scene she encounters Lionel and, at first, the old confidence manifests itself:

Joan (*seizes him by the crest of his helmet from behind, so that the helmet is forced from his head and his face is revealed. At the same time she draws her sword with her right hand*):
> Suffer that end you seek!
> The Holy Virgin claims your life through me.

143

Then, however, a sudden change takes place.

(*At this moment she looks into his face. His look arrests her, she stands motionless and slowly her arm sinks.*)
Lionel: Why hesitate, withhold the stroke of death?

In reply Joan can do no more than sign to him to retreat. Schiller, the instinctive dramatist, leaves almost everything to the actress at this point of Joan's physical temptation: her emotion is shown in actions rather than words:

Joan (*turning her face away*):   Save yourself!
    I will forget forever that your life
    Lay in my power.
Lionel: I spurn your gift, turn hatred on the giver!
    I ask no quarter, we are enemies.
    Take my life as I'd take yours.
Joan: Kill me!—
    And go! Go from here!
Lionel: What is . . . ?
Joan (*hiding her face*):   O God!
Lionel (*approaching her*):
    They say that you have never spared the life
    Of any English soldier you subdued.
    Why, then, spare mine?
Joan (*raising her sword against him with a quick movement but letting it fall again instantly as she gazes into his face*):
    O, Holy Virgin!
Lionel: Why
    Call on the Virgin? She is deaf to you,
    Knows nothing of you, for the powers of heaven
    Have no part in your acts.
Joan (*in great alarm*):   What have I done?
    My vow is broken!
        (*She wrings her hands in despair.*)
Lionel (*looks at her pityingly and comes nearer*):
    Yet I pity you!
    You touch my heart and you are merciful
    To me alone. All hatred melts away.
    Who are you? Where do you come from?

Joan: Leave me! Save
        Yourself.
Lionel: So young, so beautiful! Your face
        Sears my heart and every fibre strains
        To save you. Tell me how I may. Renounce
        This dark allegiance! Throw your weapons down!
Joan: I have lost the right to bear them.
Lionel: Cast them from you!
        Quickly, follow me.
Joan (*with horror*):   Follow—you!
Lionel: There's still time to save you. Follow me,
        Do not delay. My soul is strangely troubled,
        A longing I can give no name demands
        That I bring you to safety—
                        (*He seizes her arm.*)
Joan: Dunois is coming!
        They're looking for me. If they find you here—
Lionel: I will protect you.
Joan: If you fall to them
        Then I will die.
Lionel: Am I so dear to you?
Joan: Virgin, Queen of Heaven!
Lionel: When shall I
        See you again? When hear from you?
Joan: Never!
        Never again.
Lionel: I take this sword as pledge.
                (*He wrests the sword from her.*)
Joan: Are you beside yourself? You dare do that?
Lionel: I yield now to their force. We'll meet again.
                                  (Act III, Sc. X)

This scene has been quoted at length to demonstrate its
theatrical power. Its dramatic power, however, is more
doubtful, since the suddenness of Joan's emotion, and Lionel's
reciprocation of it, conflict with the implied realism of the play:
at best it becomes mere melodrama. The same must be said of
the *coup de théâtre* after the coronation scene in which Joan is
unable to deny her father's accusation of witchcraft. The   145

heavenly thunder which seems to speak her condemnation is too well timed with the dialogue to be anything but a theatrical trick ill-suited to Schiller's philosophic purpose.

His intention is better served by Joan's soliloquy in Act IV, Sc. I:

> ... The tool of heaven must be blind. Blind eyes
> Alone fulfil God's work. When once you saw,
> God's shield was taken from you and the snares
> Of Hell claimed you in their power.

Here the essential difference between the 'blind eyes' of the Beautiful Soul and the conflict of the Sublime Soul is laid bare. The same distinction underlies Joan's words in Act IV, Sc. IX:

> When I still tended herds upon our hills,
> Then I was happy. There was paradise!
> Shall I see that no more? Find no more joy?

Only when Joan, like Mary Stuart, has repented her sin, does strength return to her. Yet the unhappy mixture of the philosophic and miraculous in these final scenes of her captivity and escape cannot be reconciled even by Schiller's poetry:

Joan (*falling on her knees and praying passionately*):
> O hear me, God, in this my greatest need.
> My ardent supplication rises up,
> Into Your heaven I commend my soul.
> You give the slightest web that spiders spin
> Strength that can rival galleon's rigging, make
> By infinite power a cobweb's frail endurance
> From bands of iron. If it be Thy will
> These chains will fall, these towering walls burst open.
> Blind Samson—in captivity and mocked
> By proud and bitter foes—received your help.
> Trusting in You, he pitted all his strength
> Against the imprisoning pillars, till they fell.
> The mighty building crashed—

Soldier: The day is ours!

Isabeau: What's that?
Soldier: The king is taken!
Joan (*jumping up*):   Help me, God!
(*She has seized her chains with both hands and broken them. At the same time she throws herself on the soldier nearest to her, snatches his sword from him and hurries out. All gaze at her with blank astonishment.*)

(Act V, Sc. XI)

Despite such weaknesses, Goethe considered *The Maid of Orleans* Schiller's greatest artistic achievement in the theatre. Certainly in Joan's last words:

The pain is short, the joy will last forever!

(Act V, Sc. XIV)

—we see the Idealism of Schiller's thought condensed into one unforgettable line. Joan's temptation and her demonstration of moral potential are adequate poetic images of the conflict he intended to portray in all his later tragedies, but the melo- drama of the action prevents the play's ranking with either *Mary Stuart* or *Tell*.

The first performance of *The Maid* in Weimar (it had already been given in Leipzig) demonstrated, probably for the first time, the complete success of the two poets' insistence on the actors' portraying 'Ideal Beauty' on the stage. Joan was played by Amalie Wolff–Malcolmi—the fact that Jagemann was the Duke's mistress made her unsuitable for the part, because it was felt that the audience would be reminded of Voltaire's *La Pucelle*. Whereas the Leipzig performance had stressed the spectacle and ignored the poetry, Weimar underlined the idealism. True, a new cloak was bought for the coronation scene (an almost unheard of extravagance!) but the opulence of Iffland's later production in Berlin (1801) was neither attempted nor considered desirable. None the less, Iffland's production must have been memorable, for it is reported that more than eight hundred actors appeared in the fourth act and that the audience was ecstatic.[6] Schiller did not entirely approve but

[6] See Kindermann, *op. cit.*, vol. V (1962), p. 230 and note p. 725.

had given Iffland the hint for such extravagance in his stage direction to Act IV, Sc. VI:

Flute-players and hautboys open the procession. Children follow, dressed in white and bearing branches. Behind them two heralds, then a procession of halberdiers. Municipal officers in full robes follow, then two marshalls with the mace, the Duke of Burgundy carrying the sword, Dunois with the sceptre, other nobles with the crown, the Imperial Orb and Staff of Justice. Others still with offerings. Behind them knights wearing the decorations of their orders, choirboys with the thurible and two Bishops with the ampulla for the Holy Oil. The Archbishop carrying the crucifix is followed by Joan with the banner. She walks with sunken head and uncertain step. As they see her, her sisters express astonishment and joy. Behind Joan comes the King under a canopy carried by four barons. Courtiers follow and soldiers bring up the rear. When the procession is in the church the martial music ceases.

The Bride of Messina

Schiller's next play, *The Bride of Messina* (1802–3), reveals a conscious attempt to resolve the conflict of the Sensuous and Ideal elements in drama by means of the Chorus. The prefatory essay on *The Use of the Chorus in Tragedy* begins:

A poetic work must justify itself and where the deed does not speak, the word will not help greatly.

In this case, however, the 'deed'—the play itself—is less impressive than the essay, which is one of Schiller's major contributions to dramatic theory.

He takes up a position somewhere between Dr. Johnson and Bertolt Brecht. He would seem to agree with Johnson's view that:

It is false, that any representation is mistaken for reality.
(Preface to Shakespeare, 1765)

But like Brecht he seeks a form of theatre in which illusion is deliberately separated from philosophic comment. This separation he sees as the essential function of the Chorus:

The Chorus . . . purifies the tragic poem in that it separates reflection from action and, even as it does so, arms itself with poetic power.

French theatre had reduced the Chorus to colourless confidants, thus making them more naturalistic but robbing them of their ability to comment meaningfully on the action. He now seeks a theatre which makes fewer concessions to naturalism, where the Chorus comments independently and, because of the beauty of its own words, raises the level of the language throughout the play.

Conscious as always of the religious nature of Tragedy, he sets his story (the only one among his later plays which he invented entirely for himself) in Messina at a time when Greek religion, Christianity and 'Moorish superstition' were co-existent. There is an echo of Lessing's Nathan in the words which end the preface:

Under the husk of all religions lies religion itself, the Idea of the Divine, and the poet must be allowed to express this in whatever form he finds most convenient and suitable.

Unfortunately the plot, too, recalls Lessing by reminding us too forcibly of 'dramatic algebra'. Don Manuel and Don Cesar, two warring Princes of Messina, are reconciled by their widowed mother, Donna Isabella. Both have fallen in love, unknown to each other, with a young convent novice, Beatrice. When Cesar discovers his brother with Beatrice the old feud breaks out again and Manuel is killed. Too late, Don Cesar discovers that Beatrice is his own sister—Isabella had concealed the child on being warned by a dream of her husband's that:

> She would kill both his sons and all his line
> Would be destroyed in her. (Act II, Sc. V)

Another dream of her own, however, had promised Isabella that she would:

> . . . bear a daughter
> Who would heal up the warfare of my sons
> In radiant warmth of love. (*Ibid.*) 149

The irony of the play rests on the fact that both prophesies are fulfilled: its weakness is that this end is achieved by over-stressed coincidence. In short, the separation of the Sensuous and Spiritual in this play, despite the excellence of Schiller's reasoning in the essay, defeats its own end. He had aimed at a tragedy like *Oedipus* in which the characters should be set against a background of overwhelming Fate that manifested itself by oracular utterance. In the outcome the Fate seems contrived and the oracles melodramatic. Only in the utterances of the Chorus, as they comment on this tale of murder and potential incest, do we sense the Universal—the true note of Tragedy:

1st Chorus (*Cajetan*):
> Through the streets of the cities
> Disaster comes striding,
> Pursued by lament.
> Tapping today on
> This man's threshold,
> That man's tomorrow—
> Never a house that it will spare.
> Tidings unlooked for,
> Bringing disaster,
> Early or late
> Are destined by Fate
> For all who earthly existence share.

(*Berengar*) When dead leaves flutter
> In Autumn's breath,
> And dotards totter
> To palsied death,
> We see Nature obey
> Peaceful sway
> Of ancient laws
> That were hers from birth.
> Here, then, man may find no cause
> For fear!
> > But learn that life on earth
> Harrows the living with monstrous affliction!
> With violent hand

> Murder will ravage the holiest bond,
> In his Stygian hold
> Death enfold
> Even youth in his cold jurisdiction.
> *(Cajetan)* When towering clouds engulf all heaven,
> When dark-echoing thunders call,
> Every human heart is riven,
> All acknowledge Destiny's thrall.
> Even from a cloudless sky
> Comes the thunder's flashing blaze,
> Therefore in your halcyon days
> Fear deceitful Destiny.
> Do not hang your heart on gain
> That tinges life with transient hues:
> He who has, must learn to lose,
> He who is happy, must meet pain.   (Act IV, Sc. IV)

In the Weimar production, Goethe distributed the choruses of the fourth act amongst individual speakers, choosing their voices so that they contrasted yet made a harmonious whole. In directing the play, he must have been reminded of his own *Iphigenia* which, *en revanche*, Schiller directed at Weimar. Not only do both plays deal with the oracular and the struggle of human beings against Fate, both hint at the problem of agnosticism. In Goethe's play this is close to the core, in Schiller's more peripheral. Yet Isabella comes near to doubting the Gods:

> Why should I care now if the Gods reveal
> Themselves as liars, or make good their claim
> To Truth? They have done their worst with me,
> And I defy the heavens to strike more hard
> Than they have struck.   (Act IV, Sc. V)

Even Don Cesar fails to achieve Sublimity at the end of the play. True, he repents of killing his brother and there is something of the attitude we expect from a Schillerian tragic figure when he cries:

151

L

> Free death alone can break the chains of Fate.
>
> (Act IV, Sc. VIII)

But his death is tinged with the envy which he confesses has poisoned all his life. He says to Isabella:

> Can you believe I'll let my brother bear
> Advantage in his death? Let him assume
> The higher place your suffering awards him?
> Death has a cleansing charm to clarify
> Mortality in his eternal halls,
> Consume the stains of weakness till they turn
> To purest virtue, diamantine bright.
> And he, in his nobility, will stand
> As far above me as the stars from earth!
> If envy sundered us when we were brothers,
> Then it will gnaw forever at my heart
> Now he has gained eternity and lives
> Beyond all strife, to wander like a God
> Among the memories of living men.   (Act IV, Sc. IX)

Thus the ending of the play strikes us as different from that of *Mary Stuart* and *The Maid*. Mary overcomes her sinful nature, so, after her struggle of the third and fourth acts, does Joan. But Isabella seems to lose her faith and Cesar retains his envy. It is not that Schiller is negating his own theories, rather that he is portraying them in a new light—the light of human experience rather than that of philosophic calm. In the earlier plays we see only the calm at the heroine's death, here human imperfection is co-existent with it. The victory of Cesar is only partial—his motives are mixed. It was such mixed motivation which Schiller was to explore more deeply in his last completed play.

Wilhelm Tell

Critics have become so accustomed to regarding Mary Stuart and Joan as 'typical' protagonists of Schillerian drama, that many find Tell an unsatisfactory figure, seeing in him only a national hero. Annual performances in Switzerland, at Altdorf and Interlaken, encourage this partial view by cutting the controversial Parricida scene at the end, thereby presenting only one side of Tell's development. Running through the play is the thought that murder, whatever its justification, remains murder. The Swiss patriots are blind to this, constantly voicing their determination to free themselves from Austrian domination without wanton bloodshed, yet ultimately accepting Tell's shooting of Gessler unquestioningly. Walter Fürst, for example, declares:

> What must be done
> To uphold the law we'll carry out. No more!
> We'll hound the bailiffs and their lackeys, break
> Their fortresses wide open—but we'll shed
> No blood unless we must. (Act II, Sc. II)

Later he congratulates Melchtal on having saved the life of Landenberg, the Austrian Bailiff, who had blinded Melchtal's father:

> May God
> Bless you for keeping victory unstained
> By wanton blood. (Act V, Sc. I)

In the same scene Stauffacher, having learned that the Austrian Emperor has been murdered by his power-lusting son, congratulates the Swiss on their own innocence:

> They have gained
> Nothing from their outrage. Our hands, though,
> Are pure and we may pick the fruit of blessing
> Grown from this deed of blood.

In contrast to such men stands the figure of Tell. It is significant that from the beginning of the play he is shown as a lone wolf, a man who is willing to save the life of his compatriot, Baumgarten, by rowing him across the storm-tossed lake, but who steadfastly refuses to enter the world of political discussion:

153

> I've no time
> For such deliberation. When you need
> Action call on *me*—and I'll be there. (Act I, Sc. III)

Although the historical sources which Schiller used (Tschudi's sixteenth-century *Chronicon Helveticum* and Johannes Müller's *History of the Swiss Federation*) indicated that Tell was present on the Rütli when the Swiss uprising was planned, the play makes his absence conspicuous. Baumgarten comments on it in Act II, Sc. II, and Tell later informs his wife, Hedwig:

> I wasn't on the Rütli—but I shan't
> Refuse my country when she calls. (Act III, Sc. I)

So remote is Tell from political affairs that, when the Austrian hat is erected in Altdorf and the Swiss are required to do obeisance to it, he quietly ignores the symbol of the oppressors, treating it for the trumpery it is:

Walter: Look at the hat up there!
Tell: What's it got to do with us? Come on. (Act III, Sc. III)

Only when he is taken prisoner for this offence and forced by Gessler, the Austrian bailiff, to shoot an apple from his son's head as punishment, is Tell compelled to consider motives as well as action. He realises that if Gessler is allowed to live, then his own family will be further persecuted. He can no longer assume that mere physical strength and courage will be enough for him to offer the Swiss cause. He is in the position of a man who receives conflicting moral commandments: 'Thou shalt not kill' and 'Thou shalt protect thy family'. Yet the second cannot be fulfilled without transgressing the first. In such a case of conflicting Absolutes, only Understanding can decide. Tell becomes, despite himself, a 'political' figure, trapped like Elizabeth, Philip and Wallenstein into making pragmatic decisions. He is unlike such figures, however, in his very acute recognition of the need to act morally on all occasions. He sees the essential difference between temporal and eternal law and

his soliloquy when he lies in wait for Gessler at Küssnacht
insists on this:

> I lived in peace, harmed no-one, raised my bow
> Only against the wild-life of the woods.
> No murder stained my thought till you alarmed
> The covert of my peace. You turned the milk
> Of meditation into serpent's venom.
> . . . .
> My guiltless children, my beloved wife
> Must be protected from your spite.
> . . . .
> You are my Lord, you are my Emperor's bailiff.
> The Emperor, himself, would not defy
> Heaven as you do. He commissioned you
> To speak for Justice here. And sternly, too,
> To suit his anger. But he did not licence
> Unbridled, wanton, murderous lust. The living
> God demands such evil be avenged.
> . . . .
> Each traveller must journey on the way
> Of his appointed task. My own—is murder.
> In other days, when I set out, the boys
> Rejoiced to see me home. I never came
> Without some gift—a glistening alpine-flower,
> Rare bird, perhaps, or fossiled ammonite
> Such as all wanderers through the mountains find.
> Today, though, I must seek a different quarry,
> Lurk by the way consumed with murderous thoughts
> To wipe out infamy. Yet still my thoughts
> Are of my children. Nature, herself, demands
> Their innocence be shielded from your violence.
> For them alone I stretch my bow to murder.
>
> (Act IV, Sc. III)

Nowhere does Tell avoid the fact that he must commit murder.
This is the point of the controversial Parricida scene (Act V,
Sc. II) when Johannes, Duke of Swabia, seeks shelter in Tell's
house after murdering his father, the Emperor. Johannes has

killed for political ambition, Tell in obedience to the commands of Justice. Yet both are murderers.

The difficulties of this scene are two: the fact that Johannes, though clearly an important character in the play, has never been seen before; and the fact that much of Tell's dialogue seems at first sight to reduce him to self-righteousness. Although it was clearly Schiller's original intention to contrast a 'justifiable' murder with an unjustifiable one, close examination of the text suggests, however, that he has done more than this.[7] Bearing his previous soliloquy in mind, we notice that in the very moment when he declares to his wife that he can raise the hand which killed Gessler 'to heaven with impunity', it is doubtful if he, in fact, does so. Schiller frequently inserts stage directions where the text has already made them abundantly clear and, in this case, a quite different action is demanded of Tell:

(*The monk makes a sudden movement and Tell becomes aware of him.*)

It would almost seem that Schiller intended the Monk (Johannes Parricida in disguise) to halt Tell's gesture of implied total innocence.

In the ensuing duologue Tell at first rejects his visitor:

> Do you dare
> Confuse the bloody guilt of greed, ambition,
> With what the laws of justice led a father
> To do in self-defence? Did you protect
> Your children? Guard the sacred rights of home?
> Ward off the last and worst of all disaster
> From those you loved? No. I can raise my hands
> To heaven free of guilt, pronounce my curse
> On you and what you did. For I avenged
> Nature herself. Her holy cause. And you
> Defiled her. I share nothing with you. You
> Murdered. I defended all I hold
> Most dear.   (Act V, Sc. II)

Yet we know from the soliloquy that Tell is aware that his own

---

[7] Cf. William F. Mainland's introduction to his edition of *Wilhelm Tell* (Macmillan, 1968).

deed is also murder. The distinction he attempts to draw between himself and Johannes is only a partial one. A few lines later we discover that he is equally inexact in his statement 'I can . . . pronounce my curse on you and what you did'. Far from cursing Johannes, he is moved to pity him:

> I pity you,
> God knows, I pity you. So young . . . and born
> So nobly. Grandson to my Emperor Rudolf
> Come here a murderer, fleeing his pursuers,
> Racked by the doubt that lies in murder's wake
> And come to *me* . . . to my poor house . . . for help.
> (*He hides his face.*)

Is it merely to hide his tears that he covers his face? Or is it not rather that we are to be reminded that he, too, knows the horror and doubt implicit in murder? Schiller, the poet, is anxious to stress the moral difference in the two men, but Schiller, the dramatist, hints constantly at their inescapable likeness. Here, though, dramatist and poet are not in conflict as they sometimes were in the earlier plays. The one supports the other by stressing complementary aspects of the situation. Critics who have concerned themselves more with Schiller's poetry than his drama have frequently missed the subtlety of Tell's characterisation at this point, condemning the scene as poor theatre. But the apparent total innocence of Tell, implied by his longer speeches, must be set against his other remarks, the stage directions and his character as revealed in earlier scenes.

Other scenes in *Tell* have always been recognised as supremely successful in the theatre. The storm scene in Act I is full of quickly developed and sharply contrasted action. The apple-shooting is skillfully managed, thanks largely to the uniting of the Tell story with the underplot of Berta and Rudenz. In the previous acts Rudenz, the young Swiss nobleman, has seemed a traitor to his country. In love with Berta von Bruneck, a rich Austrian heiress, he sides with the oppressors. It is at the moment when Tell takes aim for the second

157

time (his courage having failed him at the first attempt) that
Rudenz announces his change of heart to Gessler and the assembled crowd:

Rudenz: I forsook my people,
            Denied my blood and wrenched the bonds of nature
            To join with you, believing that I furthered
            The best, by strengthening the Emperor's power.
            My eyes are opened. Horrified, I gaze
            At the abyss to which you led me. You deceived
            My judgement's freedom, you decoyed my heart,
            Till good intention almost made me bring
            My people to perdition.
Gessler: Will you dare
            Use this tone to me—your Lord?
Rudenz: My Lord
            And Master is the Emperor! Not you!
            I was born free as you and rate myself
            Your equal in the qualities of knighthood.
            Were you not sent here in the Emperor's name—
            A name I honour though its servants shame it—
            I'd throw my gauntlet down, requiring you
            To answer by the laws of chivalry.
            Yes! Call your troopers.
                    (*indicating the people*)
                                    I am not like *them*
            Unarmed. My sword is here. If anyone
            Dares approach me. . . !
Stauffacher (*shouting*):
            Look! The apple's fallen!
(*While all have been occupied with Rudenz's side of the stage and Berta
has thrown herself between him and the bailiff, Tell has fired the arrow.*)
                                            (Act III, Sc. III)

Thus a significant development in Rudenz's character is used
to make both a rhetorical climax, and also to prepare the
necessary stage-business (Tell's palming of the arrow) for the
greater climax of the shooting itself. Similar, if less sensational,
sureness of dramatic technique is evinced by the Rütli scene

with its contrast of characters (Stauffacher, Melchtal, Rössel-mann) its conflict of Cantonal loyalties and its varied lighting effects.

The play was first produced at Weimar on 3 March 1804. At this time, when the German lands were so heavily threatened by Napoleon, the themes of national unity and independence made an instant appeal to the audience. Attinghausen's dying appeal to the Swiss:

> Hold fast!
> Hold fast together always! Let no place
> Where freedom dwells be stranger to the rest,
> But set high-watch upon the mountain-tops
> That brotherhood be joined to brotherhood. . . .
> United! . . . Stay united!   (Act IV, Sc. II)

—seemed to have direct application to the German people. Its message appeared to be reinforced by Rösselmann's formula for the Rütli oath:

> We seek a single brotherhood of men
> Inseparable in danger and in need.   (Act II, Sc. II)

In later times (during the Franco-Prussian war, for example, and in the Nazi era) the play has also been regarded as Schiller's hymn to German patriotism. Yet it has also, it is worth noting, been banned on occasions for its outspoken pleading for demo-cracy and its treatment of the theme of regicide. All such considerations, however, have very little to do with what Schiller actually wrote and intended. His theme is Freedom, not narrow patriotism or revolutionary anarchy, and his setting is unmistakably Swiss.

This Swiss setting, with its demand for views of 'the high rocky coast of Lake Lucerne' (Act I, Sc. I), 'high mountains and beyond them still higher ice-covered peaks' (Act II, Sc. II) and 'The ravine near Küssnacht' (Act IV, Sc. III), certainly suggests that in writing the play Schiller was thinking of actual landscapes rather than painted scenery. This fact, together with the opportunities for horsemanship which it affords,   159 make *Tell* particularly suited to out-door performance. In Weimar, naturally, the scenery had to be depicted on painted backcloths, though particular care was taken—as always—to see that actors did not come into such close contact with them that the illusion of perspective was destroyed. The effect of sunrise at the end of the Rütli scene was comparatively simple: lights in the wings could be deflected from the stage to give the illusion of night at the beginning and re-directed towards the action at the appropriate moment, coloured filters of oiled paper being used to give the effect of dawn. Inevitably, however, the stress in the Weimar production was on the poetic rather than the spectacular aspects of the piece. The Shakespearean influence on Schiller allowed him to depict scenery in words, even though scenic artists reproduced those words in paint and canvas, and such speeches as Melchtal's description of his journey (Act II, Sc. II) and Tell's portrayal of the road across the Gotthard (Act V, Sc. II) are magnificent appeals to the inward eye of the audience's imagination. Despite the loving care which Weimar devoted to the speaking of such verse, however, Schiller's abiding popularity in the German theatre was not grounded on those productions, so much as on the more spectacular presentations of his plays by Iffland in Berlin— where *Tell* was presented in 1804, shortly before Schiller's death, and received with wild enthusiasm.

CHAPTER SEVEN

Goethe's Later Plays

Egmont

Goethe began *Egmont* at Frankfurt in 1775. Eleven years later, his initial period in Weimar having intervened, he took the manuscript to Italy and the play was eventually published, after many revisions, in 1788. Thus, like the final versions of *Iphigenia in Tauris*, *Torquato Tasso* and *Faust* Part I, the work exhibits a mixture of Goethe's youthful and mature approaches to drama.

The theme is the conflict of the Netherlands' patriot, Count Egmont, with the regime of Philip II at the time of the Low Countries' struggle to free themselves from Spain. Its subject-matter is, therefore, related to that of *Don Carlos*, but Goethe's play, conceived earlier than Schiller's, begins where *Don Carlos* ends. Philip sends Count Alba to Brussels to stiffen the government of the tolerant Spanish Regent, Margaret of Parma. Egmont, contrary to the advice and example of his fellow-patriot William of Orange, meets Alba. He is trapped into expressing his revolutionary sentiments, arrested and executed. A coda-like dream sequence at the end of the play hints that his death will inspire others.

The absence of action and the slightness of the story immediately mark the piece as different in genre from *Don Carlos*. Indeed, Schiller's comment on *Egmont* was:

Here is no conspicuous event, no dominating passion, no complication, no dramatic plan—nothing of all these things—but a mere putting together of several isolated actions and pictures, related to each other by almost nothing except the central character who is concerned with them all and to whom they all refer. (*On Egmont*)

Egmont does not appear until the second act. In the earlier scenes we are introduced to him as others see him. The play opens with an archery contest where the citizens of Brussels express their hatred of Spain:

> Soest: . . . We're not made like the Spaniards. We won't let them tyrannise our conscience. And the nobles must try to clip the Inquisition's wings as soon as they can. (Act I, Sc. I)

Egmont, the hero of the battle of Gravelingen, is revealed as a popular idol, loved for his courage, generosity and freedom of manner. His name is linked in the people's praises with those of Margaret of Parma and William of Orange. These three represent, each in their different ways, hope of freedom.

The second scene begins in something of the same mood as the first. Margaret enters 'in hunting-clothes, attended by courtiers, pages and servants'. It might seem that the popular sport of archery is to be paralleled by the courtly pleasure of hunting, but Margaret's first words immediately destroy the impression of the crowded stage:

> Regent: You will put off the hunt. I shall not ride today. Tell Machiavell he is to come to me.
> (*All leave.*)
> The thought of these terrible happenings leaves me no peace. (Act I, Sc. II)

Though Machiavell is not, of course, the same character as the author of *Il Principe*, his name and Margaret's concern for the revolutionary outbreaks in the Netherlands, immediately set the tone of politics seen from the point of view of the ruler. Margaret, a liberal thinker despite her intense devotion to the Church, throws new light on Egmont's character. The two figures grouped together in the popular discussion of the first scene are now contrasted. She recognises Egmont's idealism but censures his extravagance, irresponsibility and ambition. Above all, Margaret draws attention to the human problems which responsibility of ruling brings with it:

O what are we, we rulers of the earth, upon the great tide of humanity? We think we can control it but it drives us up and down, hither and thither. (*Ibid.*)

Such words clearly reflect the lessons in statesmanship which Goethe had learned at Weimar. Those lessons are even more evident in the later scene between Margaret and Machiavell, when she learns that her brother, Philip of Spain, has sent Count Alba to Brussels:

. . . He will bring a brief with him from the king. I'm old enough in the affairs of statecraft to know how people can be displaced without being deprived of their office. His first instructions will be vague. He will gain ground because he has the power. And when I complain, he will make out that he has some secret orders. When I ask to see them, he will hedge. When I insist he'll show me something else—papers referring to quite different things. And if I'm not content with that, he'll do nothing more. My words are useless. Meantime what I feared will have been done and what I desire prevented.

(Act III, Sc. I)

The humanity of Margaret's character, coupled with the fact that though she is a representative of Spain she shares some of Egmont's ideals, lends richness to the play. It is not a contrast of despotic villainy with revolutionary idealism, but a balanced comparative study of the business of government. Basically a drama of ideas rather than action, it allows us to feel the human issues raised by such ideas in dramatic cameos. Even Alba commands respect as a human being. Ruthless and inflexible, he argues from practical experience:

What kind of freedom do you want? What is the greatest freedom? —To do right!—And the king will not prevent his subjects doing it!

163

Oh, no! They think their freedom is curtailed if they're prevented from harming themselves and others. Would it not be better to give up the throne than to rule such a people? When foes threaten us from without, not a single citizen bothers himself about them, because he's only busy with his own affairs. The king demands support—the people start to quarrel amongst themselves and hence support the enemy. It is far better to restrict them, rein them in like children and lead them like children to their own best advantage. All you must realise is that a people never becomes adult or wise. A people remains childish to the end. (Act IV, Sc. II)

The contrasts and comparisons of the play are further enhanced by the scene between William of Orange and Egmont. Orange combines idealism with a sense of practical politics:

Egmont, for many years now I've borne our situation in my heart. I always stand as though looking down on a game of chess. Every movement which an opponent makes, I take to be significant. And just as idle creatures take great care to occupy themselves with the secrets of Nature, I hold it the duty and employment of a prince to know the opinions and counsels of all parties. (Act II, Sc. II)

Egmont, on the other hand, refuses all practical caution. Warned by Orange not to meet Alba, he puts his trust in the open debate of honourable minds. To refuse to meet Alba, he argues, can only lead to war. Orange accordingly advises that they return to their provinces and strengthen their forces. But Egmont counters with the slogans of romantic liberalism. 'If you have courage, no experiment is dangerous.' He insists he must 'learn to know Alba' and 'see him with my own eyes'.

Inevitably, when Egmont does meet Alba, he condemns himself out of his own mouth. It is for words not deeds that he is arrested. No specific plot is uncovered as it might have been in conventional historical drama. Goethe draws attention to the universal significance of Egmont's fall, not the particular circumstance. The passionate intensity of the hero's feeling contains a core of general democratic principle:

How often does a king show understanding? Should the people not trust many men, rather than one? Not one man, but the people themselves—the few near to the one, who have grown mature under his gaze. They alone have the right to gain wisdom.

(Act IV, Sc. II)

... the citizen wants to be ruled by someone who was born with him, educated with him and who shares the same notions of right and wrong as he does: a man he can call his brother.   (*Ibid.*)

Egmont is blindly possessed by his ideals and this possession *per se* leads to his destruction. He is aware that he is fated by his own preconceptions. On receiving a letter from his friend, Count Oliva, he rejects its admonitions with the words:

... If I were a sleep-walker, balanced perilously on a housetop, would it be kind to call my name and warn me? Wake me up and send me to my death?   (Act II, Sc. II)

He is, indeed, a kind of sleep-walker—a man who acts by inner compulsion regardless of the world around him. In a later passage from the same scene he voices his sense of mysterious predestination even more strongly:

As though whipped by unseen spirits the sun-horses of time draw on the flimsy carriage of our fate. Nothing is left to us but to take courage, hold fast the reins and guide the wheels now right, now left, away from that stone here or that deep gulley there. Who knows where we are led? We scarcely remember where we started out.

In these words, as in the whole of Egmont's character, there is a sense of paradox. Man has Free Will, it is implied, up to a certain point. He can guide the wheels of the chariot to a certain extent. Beyond this he is at the mercy of irrational forces. Egmont's decision to meet Alba is not entirely a 'free', rational one. It is partially instinctive and clearly not in the best interest of his people, since it must inevitably lead to his arrest. On the other hand it retrospectively suggests a working out of Fate's inscrutable design, since the death of an Egmont for the sake of his ideals can inspire others to action. Thus

165

Egmont's fatal decision has a poetic logic, even though it defies practical reason and Goethe shows this by the dream sequence in which Clärchen, Egmont's beloved, appears to him in prison in the guise of 'Freedom in heavenly robes'. With the accompaniment of music and by means of mime she indicates to him:

. . . that his death will procure the freedom of the provinces. She acknowledges him as a victor and offers him a crown of laurels. (Act V, Sc. IV)

Strengthened by his vision, Egmont meets his death with an apostrophe to his fellow-countrymen:

Protect your possessions! And to save your loved ones fall gladly! As I do now to give you my example.

This operatic ending cannot be considered entirely satisfactory, but the use of music and mime is significant as a further attempt to avoid particularity of words and conventional action. We are shown not the events which followed Egmont's death but rather the significance of his death. Confronted by such a passage it is tempting to dismiss *Egmont* as a prose poem rather than a play. Yet it becomes a richer experience in the theatre than the study, portraying human emotion and psychology which can only be fully realised in performance. The visual appeal of the whole is strong—the bustle of the archery contest, the appearance of Egmont to Clärchen in full Spanish costume (Act III), the constant lighting contrasts called for in the stage directions, the dramatic revelation of the soldiers in the gallery when Egmont is arrested, and the vision at the end.

It was first presented in Mainz and Frankfurt by Koch in 1789. Goethe later felt that he had outgrown the play, and only consented to its performance at Weimar in 1796 since Schiller undertook the adaptation and Iffland came as guest artist to play the lead. In the event neither Schiller's re-writing nor Iffland's performance was entirely successful. Iffland was never really suited to the subtleties of Goethe's text (he achieved a far greater triumph in the same Weimar season with Schiller's Franz Moor), and Schiller cut the text of *Egmont* severely. He removed the character of Margaret, reduced the lyricism of the language and changed lines to suggest more definite motivation. Thus, where Goethe's Egmont says to his secretary in Act II 'It all revolves around a single point: they want me to live as I do not wish to', Schiller made him say 'they want me to live as I cannot'. The change is slight but significant. Schiller's Egmont speaks as a man of practical conviction, Goethe's as a man of idealistic sensibility.[1]

In drawing the portrait of his hero, Goethe had changed the facts of history. The historical Egmont was a married man with a family—a man like Wilhelm Tell who acted to defend tangible possessions. In Goethe's play he is a bachelor with a mistress, a carefree idealist who lacks responsibilities. He thus becomes not only a more romantic figure, but one who was nearer to the situation of his author, for when Goethe first conceived the play he was ending his love affair with Lili Schönemann. Just as Weislingen and Clavigo had been images of his remorse at leaving Friederike, Egmont is made the reflection of his attitude to parting from Lili. Here, however, the stress is not on weakness, desertion and remorse, as it had been in the earlier figures, but rather on a force which compels the protagonist to act irrationally. We must remember that the break with Lili Schönemann coincided with Karl August's invitation to come to Weimar. On the one hand Goethe might have stayed in Frankfurt and become the husband of a banker's daughter. On the other he might follow his star and venture into the unknown. Like Egmont he chose the star—the apparently illogical prompting of his heart. When, at the end of his life, he reviewed this in retrospect, he recalls that he had quoted Egmont's image of 'the sun-horses' to Lili's friend, Demoiselle Delf.[2] The visionary ending of the play, therefore, reflects his intuition that his destiny was being fulfilled by his

---

[1] See Kindermann *op. cit.*, Vol. V 1962. (p. 182.)
[2] See *Poetry and Truth*, part IV, chapters XIX and XX.

M

going to Weimar, just as Egmont's destiny is fulfilled by his blind adherence to his ideals. Neither could be logically justified, both demonstrated the force of a power which Goethe termed 'daemonic'.

As Professor Peacock has shown[3] *Egmont* can be understood without reference to the theory of the 'daemonic' which Goethe expounds in *Poetry and Truth*. Since, however, the concept of the *daemonic* is more widely relevant to Goethe's approach to life, and hence to the way he depicts life on the stage, it is worth attention. Even as a young man, Goethe declares, he had been aware of a force in Nature which manifested itself in contradictions that defied reasonable explanation:

It was not divine, for it seemed unreasonable; not human, for it lacked understanding; not devilish, for it worked to good ends; not angelic, for it often betrayed malicious relish of misfortune. It resembled chance, for it showed no logical consequence; it came near to providence, for it pointed to coherence. It seemed to be able to penetrate all the barriers which confined us, to deal arbitrarily with the essential elements of our being, to condense time and to expand space. It seemed only content with the impossible, thrusting the possible from itself with scorn.

(*Poetry and Truth*, Part IV, Book XX)

Comparison is instructive with Pope's *Essay on Man*, written nearly a century earlier:

All nature is but art unknown to thee,
All chance, direction which thou canst not see;
All discord, harmony not understood;
All partial evil, universal good.

Where Pope confidently expresses Deistic rationalism, Goethe points to doubts and illogicalities. Pope writes from theory, Goethe from experience. Yet both have an underlying conviction of 'harmony'. In Goethe's case, however, the harmony is intuitively, not rationally, perceived. It exists despite the

[3] See Ronald Peacock, *Goethe's Major Plays* (Manchester University Press, 1959), p. 42.

paradoxes of man's experience and is shown to do so in his dramas.

This aspect of his theatre strikes us as modern. Time and again twentieth-century drama draws our attention to the *daemonic*—the contradictions and confusions of life which seem, nevertheless, to suggest a pattern which reason cannot confirm. We think immediately, perhaps, of *Waiting for Godot* where tantalising suggestions of an order in the universe constantly present themselves to the bewildered protagonists. We find the same feeling at the end of *Cavalcade* where Jane Marryot speaks of a '*strange* heaven' emerging from 'unbelievable hell'. In *A View from the Bridge* Alfieri senses something '*perversely* pure' in the confusions of Eddie Carbone's mind, and in *The Family Reunion* Agatha declares that:

> Accident is design
> And design is accident
> In a cloud of unknowing.

In all these cases drama is made from the same awareness of the paradoxes of life.

Iphigenia in Tauris
(1787 version, in verse)

Even in the prose version of *Iphigenia in Tauris* many of the lines show a tendency to fall into iambic pentameters. When Goethe re-cast the play into verse, he used the metrical form for dramatic as well as poetic effect: the departures from iambic metre are used to indicate changes of dramatic method. Basically the play assumes a convention of realistic conversation represented by five-beat lines. When the rhythm changes, however, the convention of action is correspondingly altered— we see the characters from within and in relationship not to each other but the Gods.

The first change in rhythmic pattern occurs at the end of Act I in Iphigenia's prayer to Diana. She has just been told by

Thoas that she must resume the rite of blood-sacrifice, yet these lines do not present her reaction realistically. Instead the speech has the effect of a Greek chorus in which the wider issue of her relationship to the accursed house of Tantalus and the Goddess Diana are expounded:

> You have clouds, most gracious of Goddesses,
> Veils to rescue the innocent victim.
> You have winds that will carry him safely
> Far from Fate's implacable hand
> Over the ocean's uttermost islands
> Where you deem it safe to conceal him.
> Wisdom shows you the ways still unknown to us,
> Past is present to you through eternity.
> Thus your eyes watch over your children
> As your light enlivens the darkness,
> Giving our planet peace and protection.
> Keep my hands free of blood, I beseech you!
> Blood that poisons hope of redemption!
> Those that we slaughter unwillingly, harrow us,
> Haunting the hours of our bitter repentance,
> Wreaking vengeance with merciless terror.
> Yet the immortals still cherish forever
> All earth's creatures that rightly revere them,
> And they lengthen the fleeting existence
> Granted to man; they reveal to his vision
> Blissful vistas of godly Olympus,
> Let him share for a moment enraptured
> Light eternal streaming from heaven.   (Act I, Sc. IV)

Yet the effect is not entirely choric and impersonal. It is a picture of Iphigenia's total being and significance, in which her immediate situation is represented only by the central line:

> Keep my hands free of blood, I beseech you.

The rest is a fuller portrait which the realistic convention could not achieve at this juncture. It may be compared to a Picasso picture in which one gets two views, full face and profile, superimposed.

Other departures from the iambic-realistic convention in the play are equally significant. In Act III Orestes is twice given half-lines, indicative not only of his intense emotion but also of the significance of what he is discussing to the pattern of destiny—a pattern which lies beyond the realistic world:

> Let strangers weave a web of lies between them,
> Let them ensnare each others' feet with tricks
> And wonted treachery. Between us two
> Let there be Truth!
> I am Orestes! This accursed head
> Has made the grave its lode-stone! I seek death!
> (Act III, Sc. I)
> From foetid vapours of her blood arose
> His mother's ghost
> And cried aloud to night's primaeval Furies: *(Ibid.)*

With such passages we may compare the laconic 'Lebt wohl!' (*Fare well*) of Thoas at the end. Once more the broken line stresses the emotion of the speaker, yet its incompleteness chorically reminds us that the Gods have left him outside the general pattern of rejoicing.

The most significant of all the metric variations in the play are those employed for Orestes' vision of Hades (Act III, Sc. II) and Iphigenia's Song of the Fates (Act IV, Sc. V). In the first, the actor finds in the four-beat lines a clue to the emotion called for in this, one of his finest scenes, in which Orestes' demented imagination conjures up the procession of his ancestors in Hades:

> Welcome, my fathers! Orestes greets you!
> The last surivor of your line:
> For what you sowed became his harvest.
> He came to hell bowed down with curses,
> And yet all burdens here are lighter.
> So take him, take him to your circle!
> I honour you, Atreus. You, too, Thyestes!
> We are all freed from hatred now.
> Show me my father. I only saw him

Once in my life!—Are you my father?
And lead my mother so lovingly with you?
May Clytemnestra give you her hand?
Why then, Orestes may approach her
And say to her 'Behold your son!'
A murderer's greeting was the certain
Watchword of our house on earth.
The house of Tantalus finds peace
Beyond the further side of night.
You call 'Welcome!'. You receive me!

But we see more than the healing of Orestes in the passage—
the will of destiny, of the Gods and the *daemonic* is being
fulfilled.

The same is true of Iphigenia's song. She remembers it
almost despite herself—she repeats these terrible words that
her nurse had taught her, praying that she may not believe
them to be true. Only if she believes the Gods are beneficent
can that beneficence work through her. This is the meaning of
her anguished cry:

Save me and save your image in my soul.

(Act IV, Sc. V)

Yet the history of her family points only to the vengeance of
destiny, the maliciousness of heaven. One of the characteristics
of the *daemonic* which Goethe observes in *Poetry and Truth*, is
its *Schadenfreude*, its relishing of others' misfortune, and this is
present in Iphigenia's words:

The feasting of gods, though,
Continues forever
At gold-laden tables.
From mountain to mountain
They stride unrelenting.
The choked breath of Titans
Exhaled in the darkness
Arises like incense
Of martyrs around them.

(*Ibid.*)

The crisis in Iphigenia is a crisis of faith. In this she is different from Schillerian heroines like Mary and Joan. Theirs is a crisis of guilt. But Iphigenia is guiltless when the play opens and must remain so to the end. How, though, can she keep her faith in the Gods, who have not only punished her family, but now torture her with a conflict of moral imperatives which resembles that presented to Wilhelm Tell? Either she must kill Orestes and Pylades, or sacrifice her redemptive purity by deceiving Thoas. Reason can supply no answer, for Reason is ultimately responsible for both dictates. She therefore turns to something one can only call Intuition—a faith in the eventual triumph of Goodness, which is as blind as Egmont's faith in his own Ideals.

There is, however, a great difference between Egmont and Iphigenia. He is a particular figure, a man firmly planted in a historical setting. Iphigenia is more universalised. We know little of her life before she came to Tauris, even her accounts of her sacrifice at Aulis and her transportation to Thoas's kingdom are vague. Diana, she says, rescued her in a cloud:

> I woke to find myself before this temple.
> (Act I, Sc. III)

> My sight grew dark—I found myself in Tauris.
> (Act V, Sc. III)

Because of this we accept Iphigenia more easily than Egmont as a poetic image of the human soul reaching out for heavenly perfection. The character itself is already a poem and the beauty of the verse which Goethe has given her makes her doubts and aspirations live with human warmth. Hers is one of the great female roles of the German stage, and in Orestes Goethe has created an almost equally impressive part for an actor.

The first production of the verse *Iphigenia in Tauris* at Weimar was undertaken by Schiller in 1802. It was not entirely successful, partially because Schiller misunderstood the nature of the

173

piece, and partially owing to the casting. Schiller wished to make the play more outwardly dramatic and suggested having the Furies appear on the stage and allowing Thoas a greater part in the action. Both suggestions were turned down by Goethe, but they reveal Schiller's basic inability to accept the piece for what it is—the inward drama of a soul. A subsequent production (1807) proved more successful and the play has found a frequent and honoured place in the repertory of the German-speaking theatre.

Torquato Tasso

Torquato Tasso was begun in Goethe's early years at Weimar, re-worked in Italy and finished after his return. Its first performance was at Weimar on 16 February 1807 with Pius Alexander Wolff in the title role.

In presenting the life and character of the sixteenth-century Italian poet on the stage, Goethe concentrates on a few simple events, to some extent rearranging the chronology of history. Tasso is shown as a young man at the Court of his patron Alphonso II of Este. In the opening scene he is crowned with a laurel chaplet in the garden of Belriguardo by the Duke's sister, the Princess, and her lady-in-waiting, Leonora Sanvitale. The Duke explains:

> This crown prefigures that which you will wear
> With future honour on the Capitol.   (Act I, Sc. III)

This recognition of Tasso's eminence as a poet was not historically planned until much later in his life and was, in fact, ultimately prevented by his death in 1595.

The coronation over, Tasso is persuaded to end his animosity to the Duke's Secretary of State, Antonio. Instead of peace, a fresh quarrel breaks out between them and Tasso draws his sword on Antonio. For this breach of etiquette he is punished by confinement to his chambers. He decides to leave Ferrara but the Princess appeals to him to return. Mistaking her veiled

174

declaration of Platonic affection for a declaration of physical love, Tasso dares to embrace her. For this second breach of etiquette, more serious than the first, he is finally banished and left at the end of the play seeking the help of his former adversary, Antonio.

The portrait of Tasso is, perhaps, the most detailed in all Goethe's dramas and presents a figure at once sympathetic and repellant. For this reason it is useful to consider first the ways in which he is made attractive to us. Our first impression is one of brilliance mingled with modesty. He at first declines the honour of the laurel and even when he receives it declares:

> The cool refreshment of this crown, reserved
> For brows of heroes, shames my little worth.
> O Gods, remove it from me and, transfigured
> Amongst the highest clouds of heaven, let
> It rise unreachable! May all my life
> Be endless pilgrimage towards its goal.   (*Ibid.*)

Throughout the play he shows a sense of dissatisfaction with his own achievements which suggests man's universal striving for perfection:

> Show me the man who has achieved in full
> What I still strive for, though! Present the hero
> Whose fame I've only known on history's page,
> Acquaint me with the poet who may dare
> Equate himself with Virgil or with Homer —
> Yes, what is more, show me the man who earned
> This prize I wear, threefold, and who would blush
> Three times as deep to carry such a crown,
> Then you will see me kneel before the God
> Who gifted me so greatly, and not rise
> Until the honour that now decks my brow
> Is lifted and transferred to his.   (Act II, Sc. III)

Even in his self-pity we detect the genuine artist's refusal to rest content with his work. He announces he will go to Rome: 175

> If I cannot complete my poem there,
> I never shall complete it. Yet I feel
> Fortune is set to frown on all I do.
> I'll change it but not bring it to perfection.
>
> (Act V, Sc. IV)

Further sympathy for him accrues from the attitude of the Court towards his art. Though the Duke is his patron and friend, it is clear that he regards Tasso as a 'possession' and to some extent only tolerates his whims for the sake of the glory he brings to Ferrara:

> He wants to leave. All right! I shall not hold him.
> He'll go! He'll go to Rome. So be it, then.
> But Scipio Gonzaga shall not filch him,
> Nor cunning Medicis make him their spoil.
> The power of Italy derives itself
> From rivalry of neighbours to possess
> And utilise the highest gifts of man.
> A Prince who fails to gather talent to him
> Is like a general dispossessed of troops.
> No matter who he be, the man whose ear
> Is dull to poetry's voice is nothing more
> Than a barbarian. I discovered Tasso,
> I chose him. I am proud to have him serve me.
> And since I did so much to ease his path
> I will not lose him lightly.   (Act V, Sc. I)

Even Leonora Sanvitale, who loves him, shows the same selfish quality in her affection. Questioning her own attitude towards him, she admits she has all she could desire in life:

> Are you not rich enough? What do you lack?
> A husband, son, possessions, rank and beauty—
> All these you have. And are you still desirous
> To add him to their number? Do you love him?
> Why else can you not bear to give him up?
> Admit it to yourself—the secret charm
> Of seeing your reflection in his soul.

Is Laura's, then, the only name to fall
In poet's cadence from all gentle lips?
And is it Petrarch only has the right
To make a goddess out of unknown charms?
Where is the man who dares compare himself
With him I feel for? He is honoured now
And all posterity will name his name.
. . . .
All that is transient he preserves in song
And you will still be beautiful, still gay
When circling Fortune long ago has torn
You to oblivion.   (Act III, Sc. III)

The elegance of her poetic imagination does not conceal the
cold self-seeking of her heart. And she continues the speech
with an analysis of the Princess's attitude which is accurate
enough and betrays in her, too, the same lack of warmth:

The inclination which she feels towards him
Is of a pattern with her other passions
Which, silent as the moon, illuminate
The traveller wanly on his nighted path.
They give no warmth and proffer him no joy
Nor sense of life's intoxicating power.
She'll be as well content to find him gone,
As happy, as she was to see him daily.

Thus, though the Duke is tolerant and generous, though the
Princess and Leonora are sensitive, cultivated and charming,
we feel all the time that Tasso is surrounded by a world that is
only superficially attuned to his poetry. He ultimately proves
too passionate a creature to live within its framework.

By showing this the play returns to the theme of *Egmont*: the
conflict between the poetic spirit and the world of affairs.
Yet Tasso's portrait is drawn more fully and realistically than
Egmont's. He is not only romantic and idealistic, but distaste-
fully self-indulgent and suspicious. As Goethe remorselessly and
accurately paints this side of him, we sometimes seem to have
wandered into a different kind of play. When, for example,   177

Antonio speaks of the poet's gluttony and hypochondria, we
could almost be listening to a passage from one of Molière's
more bitter comedies:

> Does he fulfil the first of human duties—
> To choose his food and drink—since Nature did not
> Inhibit appetite in men, as beasts?
> Is he not like a child who finds delight
> In every taste that fawns upon his gums?
> When does he mingle water with his wine?
> The richest spices, sweetmeats, heady drinks,
> One on another he will gulp them down!
> Then miserably attribute melancholia,
> Hot blood and his too violent disposition
> To Fate and Nature, both of which he curses.
> How often and how foolishly I've seen him
> Haggle with his doctor! One might laugh—
> If anything which gives another pain,
> And tortures those around him, could be laughed at.
> 'The pain is here' he murmurs anxiously
> And full of chagrin. 'What do you commend?
> Give me a remedy.' 'Right' the doctor answers
> 'Avoid this thing or that!' 'Impossible!'
> 'Very well, then, take this medicine'. 'No!
> It tastes disgusting. It revolts my nature!'
> 'Drink water, then!' 'No water! I shun water. . . .'
>
> (Act V, Sc. I)

Antonio is shown as the opposite of Tasso in the play. He is
the successful and trusted politician, a man who fits Leonora's
description of a 'character' as opposed to what she terms a
'talent' in the famous lines:

> A talent forms itself in solitude,
> A character in currents of the world. (Act I, Sc. II)

Characteristically, Goethe does not only oppose the two figures
but implies that they are complementary to each other. As
Leonora again observes:

> They are two men. I've felt so long the cause
> Of animosity between them lies
> In Nature's failing to have made them one.
> If they could only see their best advantage
> They would unite as friends. . . .   (Act III, Sc. II)

The initial attempt to bring about a *rapprochement* between them has, therefore, a symbolic significance. Yet it is also depicted with psychological depth. To Tasso's offer of friendship, Antonio, who has, himself, ambitions to be considered a poet, is coldly cautious. While not blind to Tasso's talent, he cannot refrain from hinting that he has good fortune also:

> I willingly accord you all your worth
> And all your fortune too. I merely see
> The gulf between us is too great to bridge.
> (Act II, Sc. III)

Tasso's vanity is stung. If Antonio cherishes illusions of himself as a poet, he sees himself as a man of action:

> I grant I'm young, have yet to prove myself:
> But I will yield to none in will and courage.

Antonio's reply, though just, betrays his latent envy: he alludes to the crown Tasso is still wearing:

> You cannot lure brave action by your will,
> Courage imagines every way is short:
> He who has reached the goal receives a crown
> And many worthy men miss coronation.
> Yet there are flimsy coronets and crowns
> Distinct from this. Such trinkets may be gained
> In comfort as we wander through the world.

In general, however, it is Antonio who emerges from this scene with credit. When Tasso urges his own introspective and intuitive sense of virtue against Antonio's disciplined attitude, the latter replies with one of the most trenchant criticisms of the poet in the play:

179

> No man has ever learned to know himself
> By looking inward. He will miss his measure
> And, lacking standard, judge himself too low
> Or else, alas, too high. We recognise
> Our stature only in our fellow men:
> The school of life instructs what each man is.

He goes on to taunt Tasso with the words:

> Where word-play, lyric-strings, decide the issue
> You may indeed emerge victorious.

Confronted with such home truth, Tasso draws his sword on his fellow courtier. This, and his attempt to embrace the Princess in Act V, are the only moments of action in the play. Their isolation is significant and, surely, intentionally planned. Tasso's inner nature rebels against the artificial restraints which have been laid on it, just as Goethe seems eventually to have rebelled against the Platonic discipline imposed by Frau von Stein. Yet it is important to realise that the play does not blame the conventions of Court life for Tasso's outbursts. The other characters manage to live at Court successfully, if not entirely happily. The Princess is a particular example. She, too, knows Tasso's sense of the dissatisfaction attendant on human striving:

> Indeed, the world is beautiful. Its breadth
> Quivers with living pageantry of Good.
> But yet that Good seems always to be placed
> One pace beyond pursuit, outdistancing
> Our fearful yearning step by step forever,
> Until it lures us to the final grave.
> How seldom is it man can realise
> What seemed to him once sure and pre-ordained.
> How seldom is it that his hand can hold
> What once his happy fingers sought to grasp.
> What yielded to us once, escapes abruptly:
> The hold is loosed on what we clutched with greed.

Earth offers joys, but we may know them not:
We know them well, but yet their worth escapes us.
(Act III, Sc. II)

Yet she has a self-discipline that Tasso lacks. It is his self-indulgence in introspective melancholia that conditions his outbursts, not the atmosphere of the Court. Admittedly the Princess's final declaration of 'love' for him is ambiguous

I have to leave you and my heart refuses.
(Act V, Sc. IV)

but this confusion of Platonic and physical affection is only the occasion of Tasso's act, not its cause. The cause is deeper and raises the event (like the drawing of his sword on Antonio) to something more significant than an offence against propiety.

Thus Tasso acquires a Hamlet-like complexity. He is not a symbol of the Poet, but essentially the portrait of a particular poet. Many of his judgements lack universality and he constantly misinterprets the intentions of those who try to help him. He imagines Leonora wishes him to leave Ferrara because he is disgraced and she has no further use for him; when the Duke insists he must 'learn the worth of life', he characteristically sees the words as being inspired by Antonio. Even when he speaks movingly of his own art, the impression of his preciousness is inescapable:

If I can dream no more, write no more verse,
Then life itself will be no longer life.
Would you forbid the silk-worm, then, to spin
Himself towards death? For he involves himself
In nets of splendour woven from within,
Till all is coffined close beneath their fold.
O that some kind divinity would give
That enviable fate to us: that like
The worm we might awaken to unfold
Our wings with sudden joy in unknown vales
Warmed by the southern sun.   (Act V, Sc. II)   181

Yet, like Shakespeare's Richard II, his weakness becomes a kind of strength through his poetic utterance. He is one of the few cases of a poet represented in a play, who really convinces us of his poetic gifts. The verse form of the drama, therefore, as in *Iphigenia*, becomes an essential part of its dramatic construction. It enables Goethe to present a more complex and impartial view of the total action than the basic scheme of the play would seem to allow. Basically the story of Tasso's two indiscretions and his anti-social introspection, backed up by repeated efforts of the other characters to wean him from his self-regard, put him in the wrong. Yet Tasso's power to turn his suffering into music presents another picture. Such lines as Leonora's observation that Tasso and Antonio should have been formed by Nature as one man, point to a reconciliation, which is partially achieved at the end. Yet, as Professor Peacock has shown, the quality of the poetry in Tasso's last speech is inferior to that of the earlier scenes.[4] For this reason, Peacock suggests, the ending of the play is difficult to interpret—in other words, the poetry of Tasso which has hitherto contributed so greatly to our seeing a wider vision than that suggested by the action, suddenly becomes opaque and confused.

The great difficulty of the last speech lies in the mixture of the imagery. At first Tasso seems to see himself as a wave of the sea and Antonio as a rock. Then, without warning, Tasso becomes a mariner who is shipwrecked on the wave which formerly represented himself:

> (*Antonio comes to Tasso and takes him by the hand.*)
> Tasso: You stand so strong and still in your nobility
> And I seem nothing but the storm-tossed wave.
> Consider, though, and do not overrate
> Your strength. For powerful Nature which set fast
> The rock, endowed the wave with mutability.
> When Nature sends her storm, the wave flies forth,
> Trembles, swells and bows its head in foam.
> On that bright undulation, where the sun

    [4] Peacock, *op. cit.*, pp. 115–16.

14

17

18

Once saw his own reflection, on that breast
Where all the stars were lulled to gentle sleep
The sheen is dimmed, the peace is put to flight.
Now danger looms, I do not know myself.
Yet now I dare confess it without shame.
The helm is shattered and the ship is cracked
In every side. The earth beneath my feet
Bursts open. I stretch out my arms to you.
The mariner at last must clutch the rock
Which Destiny once marked for his destruction.

(Act V, Sc. V)

The confusion of imagery is certainly puzzling, suggesting a confusion in Goethe's own attitude to the end of the play. It is clearly his intellectual intention to point the moral that Tasso 'must clutch the rock', the discipline which Antonio represents. Emotionally, however, he seems to identify himself with the character of Tasso rather than with the lesson the poet has to learn. Tasso glimpses and states the universal truth. Whether he accepts it wholeheartedly as applied to himself, is perhaps another matter. Had Schiller painted his portrait, one feels the ending of the play would have been as positive, as unambiguously self-committed as Joan's:

The pain is short, the joy will last forever.

But Goethe does not dissolve his hero in moral abstraction. As though unwilling to present the mercurial and complex character of Tasso as completely attuned to the moral of the piece, he fidgets from image to image. Yet though the quality of the poetry is impaired, the uncertainty of the dramatist's attitude suggests (perhaps fortuitously) the confusion in Tasso, himself, and hence the lines are effective on the stage.

Tasso is not a play for a large theatre, but rather the dramatic equivalent of chamber music, suggesting in some ways the great plays of Chekhov. It is one of Goethe's supreme achievements: a work of strange contradictions, a juxtaposing of idealism and reality, which fascinates us more at each new acquaintance.

The Natural Daughter

Originally planned as an opera, *The Natural Daughter* was eventually turned into a spoken drama and first performed at Weimar in 1803. It is the first part of an unfinished trilogy on themes suggested by the French Revolution, but since the remaining parts were never written and Goethe's notes throw little light on their intention, judgement is difficult even on that part of the work which we possess. The plot concerns a Duke who, after the death of his mistress, recognises the birth-right of his illegitimate daughter, Eugenia—a girl who has been brought up as a 'child of nature'. Her half-brother is jealous of her claims and Eugenia's Stewardess is persuaded to abduct her—a hunting accident being used as a pretext for her 'death'. The Stewardess, however, realises that her mistress can be saved by a bourgeois marriage which would automatically rob her of her title. Such a marriage is arranged at the end of the play, though Eugenia secures a promise from her husband that it shall not be consummated.

The relationship with the French Revolution is a distant one: themes of aristocratic rule, bourgeois worth, despotism and political chaos are discussed as universal issues in an abstract setting. Besides these we have other themes that are less clearly formulated. We can only speculate on such questions as to whether Eugenia's apparent death is to prelude some idea of 'resurrection', and whether the agreement that her husband shall regard her only as a sister betokens the fact that she is to become a kind of second Iphigenia.

Apart from Eugenia, none of the characters are given names, being delineated only as 'King', 'Duke', 'Secretary' and so on. Although the stage direction for Act III reads:

The Duke's antechamber: richly furnished, modern.

the general impression is of timelessness. The final effect is nearer to that of *The Winter's Tale* or *The Tempest* than a play on a political theme. The piece has been performed with some measure of success in twentieth-century Germany, largely owing to the beauty and strength of some of its verse, which equals that of *Tasso* and *Iphigenia*. It also provides opportunities for the actors, in such passages as the Duke's frenzied grief for the loss of his daughter:

> Then let the swollen flood
> Destroy its dams and turn the land to sea,
> The turbulent ocean open all her gulfs
> To swallow cargoes, stately crafts and crews!
> Let ranks of war spread far across the globe
> And pile on bloody pastures death on death!
>
> (Act III, Sc. II)

But the fragmentary nature of the whole proved so confusing to the first audience that the play failed. Goethe wrote nothing more for the stage except the short allegorical spectacle *Epimenides' Awakening* which Iffland requested for Berlin after the fall of Napoleon. This masque-like piece, which shows Love and Faith chained by Oppression and finally rescued by Hope, and which concludes with a choric hymn to the freed German peoples, was presented again in Weimar on 30 January 1816. Significantly this later presentation reduced the masses of soldiery called for in the text to a few symbolic figures. 'The rest' Goethe observed 'might be imagined.'

Faust

Goethe began Faust in 1773 and worked on it until his departure for Weimar. This early version was not published in his lifetime but a transcription of it made by Fräulein Göchhausen, one of the ladies at the Weimar Court, was subsequently rediscovered and published in 1887. This version of the play is known as the *Urfaust (original Faust)* and opens with the scene in Faust's study. It concerns itself chiefly with the Faust–Gretchen story, which here ends with Gretchen's being condemned for the murder of her illegitimate child. No 'Voice from Above' announces her salvation as in the final version of Part I.

In 1790 Goethe published *Faust: A Fragment* (which added two scenes to the original draft) and in 1808 *Faust, Part I*. *Faust, Part II* was not completed until 1831 and not published until after the poet's death, although the Helen scenes had come out in 1827. The whole, therefore, is a piecing together of fragments on which Goethe had worked for over fifty years, and, as might be expected, exhibits a great variety of styles. Part I has a long history of successful performance, but Part II, though sometimes staged as a Festival Piece in modern Germany, is nearer to a poem than a play. Its transference to the stage demands experimental production methods which cannot be properly discussed in a book concerned with history of theatre at Weimar during Goethe's lifetime. At the same time, Part II cannot be left entirely out of account since it completes the Faust story and to some extent sets Part I in perspective.

The Events of Parts I and II

In dealing with the dramatic techniques of *Faust* it is, perhaps, easiest to remind the reader of the general lines of the action and then comment on individual episodes and characters.

After the Prologue on the Stage and the Prologue in Heaven we discover Faust in his study. Wearied of the pursuit of learning he summons up the Spirit of the Earth by means of magic. Since the Earth-Spirit rejects him, however, he contemplates suicide, only to be deterred by the sound of voices greeting Easter Morning. Together with his pedantic student assistant, Wagner, he takes a walk outside the town, mingling with the common people and eventually being followed home by a stray poodle. As Faust sits in his study, struggling to translate St. John's Gospel, the poodle manifests itself as Mephistopheles. A wager is then drawn up: Mephisto shall serve Faust on this earth in the hope of claiming his soul in the hereafter. He shall only do this, however, if Faust declares he has found perfect happiness on earth. If this does not happen, Mephisto shall be deemed to have failed.

Faust's aim in making this wager is to obtain greater knowledge of the world and its inhabitants. It is not, therefore, 'learning' which he seeks but 'experience'. Mephisto is to show him first 'the small world' and then 'the large'. The remainder of Part I is concerned with the small world. Mephisto takes Faust first to Auerbach's Cellar (a favourite drinking haunt of Leipzig students) and then to the Witch's Kitchen where the Doctor is given a potion to restore his youth. Immediately following this scene, Faust meets Gretchen for the first time. He persuades Mephistopheles to help him woo her with a gift of jewellery, which is immediately surrendered by Gretchen's mother to the local priest. A second gift of jewels is concealed from the mother's eyes with the aid of Frau Martha, Gretchen's worldly minded neighbour. While Faust continues to court Gretchen, Mephisto occupies himself with Martha.

At this juncture the scene *Forest and Cavern* is inserted in the final form of the play. A late addition, it is somewhat loosely related to the dramatic structure and must be examined later in connection with the characters of Faust and Mephistopheles, together with the equally tangential *Walpurgisnacht* scene.

These episodes apart, the remainder of Part I is concerned with the Faust–Gretchen romance. Both lovers become guilty of blood: Faust, aided by Mephistopheles, kills Gretchen's brother, Valentin, in a duel. Gretchen, in order to secure a meeting with Faust, gives her mother a sleeping-draught from which she dies. When Gretchen's illegitimate child is born, she kills it and is arrested. The play concludes with the demented Gretchen in prison, unwilling to follow Faust when he comes to rescue her and finally deserted by him. As Faust and Mephisto leave, the latter announces that Gretchen has been condemned, but a voice 'from Above' announces that she is saved, despite her sins.

When Part II opens, the world of Gretchen is forgotten. Faust is discovered asleep in a flowery meadow and a chorus of spirits, led by Ariel, induce him to forget his past suffering. He goes to the Emperor's Court, where, despite political chaos and public poverty, Carnival is celebrated with a spectacular masquerade. Mephisto introduces paper money, ostensibly backed by the unmined treasures of the earth, as a solution to the kingdom's poverty. At first delighted with his inflationary wealth, the Emperor tires of it and requests Faust to use his magic to summon up the spirits of Helen and Paris: the classic forms of female and male beauty. It is a request that Mephisto cannot easily fulfil—the classical world is not his concern—and Faust has to journey alone to 'The Mothers', mythical beings who will help him in his quest. On his return, he conjures up the spirits of Paris and Helen, but as he impetuously tries to embrace the figure of Helen, she disappears.

In the second act of Part II we are reintroduced to Wagner, who now occupies Faust's old study and has succeeded in creating *Homunculus*, a form of artificially created life which remains imprisoned within the phial that gave it birth. Thus Homunculus immediately suggests Faust's own situation, for both are striving for higher freedom. It is Homunculus who leads Faust and Mephisto to the Classical *Walpurgisnacht*, a companion scene to the Witches' Sabbath in Part I, yet one that is markedly different in tone. There all was chaos and vulgarity, here all is ordered, beautiful and disciplined. Homunculus sees Galatea (another representation of idealised Beauty) and in rapture of love for her dashes himself to death against her shell-chariot.

In Act III Faust meets Helen once more. She is presented as the innocent victim of the Trojan War, who longs only to fulfil her husband's command that she should prepare a sacrifice. Mephistopheles, who has temporarily assumed the likeness of Phorkyas, the embodiment of Ugliness, reveals that in giving this command, Menelaus intended Helen, herself, to be the victim. As a means of escaping her fate, Mephisto urges marriage with Faust. Helen agrees and is transported in a mist to Faust's castle. After his defeat of Menelaus' army, Faust

188

becomes father to Helen's child, Euphorion, a figure who thus symbolises poetry and art born from the union of Nordic genius with Classical beauty. (In more particular terms, Euphorion suggests Lord Byron, whose work has something of the mixture of 'Classicism' and 'Romanticism' we find in Goethe's own, and whose death on his way to fight for the cause of Greek freedom, greatly moved the German poet.) Like Faust, Euphorion is a restless spirit who longs to make himself master of all human experience, cost what it may to himself and others:

Helen, Faust and Chorus: Would you emulate the deer?
                            What if you should miss the ledge?
Euphorion: I must climb to heights more sheer,
                            I must view earth's farthest edge.
                                                        (*Shady Grove*)

Unable to accept the peace of his parental home, he attempts, like Icarus, to fly, but falls dead at his parents' feet. For a moment, says the stage direction, we seem to recognise in him 'a well-known figure' (Byron), then:

. . . *the physical body disappears immediately, the aureola rises like a comet to heaven, leaving only the tunic, cloak and lyre on the ground.* (*Ibid.*)

Euphorion's voice is heard from the distance, begging his mother not to leave him alone in the realms of darkness. When the Chorus have mourned the loss of the poet, Helen turns to Faust with the words:

Alas, an ancient word foretells my fate as well,
For Beauty may not dwell eternally with Joy.
The ties of life are torn, the bonds of love unskeined
And as I mourn for both, I bid farewell in woe
And seek no more the warmth and solace of your arms.
Persephone, receive his spirit and my own.

(*She embraces Faust, her body disappears, her dress and veil remain in his arms.*)   (*Ibid.*) 189

The fourth act brings us back to the Emperor's Court. Faust, again aided by Mephisto, who has now abandoned his 'classical' disguise of Phorkyas, defeats the enemies of the empire and is rewarded by a gift of land. Principally a satire on corrupt government, the act repeats many of the themes already handled in Act I of Part II and lacks strong dramatic interest.

In Act V, however, we have material of more dramatic significance. Faust, now about a hundred years old, tries to establish a Utopia on the land which the Emperor has given him. The task is almost complete, but the dwelling of an old couple, Philemon and Baucis, who have charge of a small chapel, must still be demolished if perfection is to be achieved. At first Faust hesitates to expel the pair, but Mephisto persuades him to do so. Their hut is destroyed by fire and they perish. Too late, Faust repents the inhumanity of his act. He is visited by allegorical figures: Want, Guilt, Need and Care. Since he is now a rich man the first three soon depart, but Care enters his palace and blinds him. He taps his blind way to the great courtyard in front of the palace, where Mephistopheles and the Lemures (evil spirits of the dead) are digging his grave. Imagining the sound of their digging to be that of workmen engaged on completing his Utopia, he seems at last to have found contentment. He echoes the words of his original wager with Mephisto in the Study Scene of Part I and, as he sinks to the ground, the Lemures seize him. Despite Mephisto's apparent triumph, however, Faust's soul is saved. The heavenly hosts descend, pelting Mephisto with roses, the symbols of love, which turn to fire as they strike him. The angels bear 'the immortal part of Faust' to heaven, where God Himself is significantly not depicted. Even in the Prologue in Heaven of Part I, we meet not 'God', but only the figure called 'The Lord'. This refusal to represent the Deity on the stage is not so much indicative of Goethe's unwillingness to offend religious sensibility (though his objections to the Communion scene in *Mary Stuart* suggest he was cautious in such matters), but springs rather from his sense that Ultimate Truth cannot possibly be represented by a particular image. The figures of Goethe's heaven are representative of different aspects of idealised Truth which, when taken together, give some notion of the Ultimate Whole. Even Faust is not directed to appear in the scene. We meet first the Anchorites, then the Pater Ecstaticus, the Pater Profundus, the Pater Seraphicus, the Angels, and finally the Mater Gloriosa with three penitents (Mary Magdalen, the Woman of Samaria and Mary of Egypt) kneeling before her. With these is another penitent 'formerly known as Gretchen'. It is she who declares that her beloved has been returned to her and that his trials and torments are now over. The play concludes with the final song of the *Chorus mysticus*:

> All that must pass away
> Proves only fable,
> All that lacks power to stay
> Here becomes stable.
> Here the inscrutable
> Lives to our sight,
> Woman immutable
> Leads to this height.

The Dramatic Method of Faust

Such a brief summary as that given above necessarily misses out many incidents in the work, but serves to remind us of the connections between the two parts. Particularly important to the dramatic design of the whole is the connection between the 'Prologue on the Stage' and the final *Chorus Mysticus*.

The Prologue on the Stage (though a late addition to Part I) sets the tone and character of the play. It is a dialogue between the Theatre Director, the Poet and a 'Merry Person'. In many modern productions these roles are taken by the actors who subsequently play Faust (the Poet), Mephisto (the Merry Person) and the Lord (the Theatre Director). Certainly the arguments advanced suit this double casting: the Poet is full of lofty inspiration; the Merry Person asks only to be amused, the Theatre Director asks for 'the whole circle of creation' to be presented on stage. Yet the purpose of this Prologue is not only to introduce us to the themes and characters of the work, it turns all that follows into a play-within-a-play.

Thus the next scene, the Prologue in Heaven, uses the conventions of the medieval stage and the travelling-booth theatres of the second half of the eighteenth century. We are not asked to believe that heaven is like this, merely to accept it as a theatrical representation of heaven. The rhyming couplets, reminiscent of the plays of Hans Sachs, reinforce the illusion: what we witness is only a shadow of ultimate reality. This is the point which is made by the *Chorus Mysticus* at the end. The transient forms of life are only a parable, an Image of the Ideal which man cannot depict in concrete terms.

The whole of Part II is an attempt to hint at the nature of Ideal Reality by means of showing the inadequacy and impermanence of particular symbols. Hence even Helen vanishes in Faust's embrace, and Art, represented by Euphorion, is doomed to ultimate destruction. The key to the dramatic pattern of the second part lies in the dialogue between Faust and Mephisto concerning the Mothers. These guardians of Ultimate Truth and Beauty lie beyond the world of sense-perception. Even, Mephisto insists, if we try to imagine the greatest loneliness it is possible for man to experience, we cannot picture their world. They live in the realm of the inscrutable:

Mephisto: The pagan world's not my concern.
　　　　　Their Hades is not housed in Hell.
　　　　　Yet there's a way.
Faust:　　　　　　　　So tell me quickly, then.
Mephisto: I fear to show what's hid from common ken.
　　　　　Goddesses sit alone, enthroned, sublime:
　　　　　No place encircles them, they know no time.
　　　　　Man may not speak of creatures so divine!
　　　　　They are the Mothers.
Faust (*startled*):　　　　　　Mothers?

Mephisto: You turn cold?
Faust: The Mothers! Mothers! Wonders manifold!
Mephisto: Truly, it is! No mortal eye may gain
               Sight of these Spirits, whom *we* fear to name.
               And you may mine the depths to reach their glade—
               Indeed, it's thanks to you we need their aid!
Faust: What is the way?
Mephisto: No way! No trace of feet
               On that untrodden path. You will entreat
               Such Goddesses in vain! Are you still keen?
               There are no locks, no bolts you may draw back.
               The bleakest solitude marks out the track.
               Can you conceive what solitude could mean?
               . . . .
               If you had swum the span of every ocean
               And gazed upon infinity,
               You'd still behold the waves' unending motion
               Though fearing still the fell calamity.
               You'd still see *something*. On the placid tide
               Of green, you'd watch the lissom dolphins glide:
               See sailing clouds, see sun and moon and stars.
               But in that empty, distant world of theirs
               You will see nothing and not hear so much
               As sound of foot-fall! Feel no sense of touch!
                                            (*Dark Gallery*)

In such passages the overtones of the verse carry most of the
weight. Yet here and in many other passages of Part II (the
deaths of Helen and Euphorion, the destruction of Homunculus,
and the moment when the blinded Faust leaves his castle, for
example) there is a strong sense of the dramatic. Difficult as
some passages are to realise on the stage, sensitive and imaginative direction might make them work in the cinema, for the
language draws our attention to specific aspects of a situation
or object, much as the film camera does, then abruptly focuses
attention on something else as a means of philosophical and
dramatic comment.

We become aware of this even in the earliest scenes of the   193

Urfaust. The Earth-Spirit might well belong to Part II, for it is through the rhythms and changing imagery of his verse that we comprehend him. At first sight he seems to live in words alone, the attempt to realise him in theatrical terms seems almost superfluous. But in fact it is not. We are made to wonder at a theatrical trick effect, and then to realise that beyond this wonder lies the greater wonder of Nature itself. It is another reminder that both the play we are watching, and life itself, are only parables of higher Truth:

> I seethe within the floods of life,
> In stormy action's wave
> I weave and wander free:
> Both birth and grave,
> Eternal sea,
> Chequered patterns changed by strife,
> Radiance of glowing life.
> I weave at the humming loom of time
> The living veil of the Divine.   (*Night*)

Use of Verse in the Play

Every episode in *Faust* has its particular speech rhythm and form. Many of the medieval scenes employ the four-beat rhyming lines of Hans Sachs, the witches speak doggerel, the Helen scenes are in hexameters, in the Gretchen episodes ballads are frequently employed. Such changes of verse must be observed both in translation and performance, for they lend a kind of chorus to the work. Through them, even when the play is at its most naturalistic and moving, we become aware of a distancing, a move from the particular to the universal.

One of the earliest examples of this is Mephisto's aside to the audience at the end of the Prologue in Heaven. In the first Prologue the couplets are used to comment on the contemporary scene, as, for example, when the Director cautions the Poet:

> Remember who you're writing for:
> One patron finds his life a bore,

> Another comes too full of food and drink.
> And what is worse, a whole lot more
> Read journalists who tell them what to think!
>
> *(Prologue in the Theatre)*

In the second Prologue the same kind of verse is used for a medieval dialogue between the Lord and Mephisto. Yet the tone of colloquial irreverence in Mephisto's final words recalls the tone of the earlier scene. Thus a sense of 'double-time' is established: the Prologue in Heaven becomes both medieval and modern:

> I like to see the Old Man now and then
> To keep relations on the level.
> I find it charming that the Prince of Men
> Should speak humanely with the very Devil.

In the Gretchen episodes the ballad-like form of the verse constantly suggests the purity and simplicity that lie behind the realistically observed triviality of her conversation. The rhyming verse transforms her from a mere peasant girl into a symbol of Purity such as one might find in a ballad or morality play, yet the particularity of Goethe's observation retains the sense of realism in her dialogue:

Faust: You are often left alone?
Margarete:[5] Yes. We've such a tiny home
            And yet I'm always on the run.
            It must be cared for—we've no maid.
            I cook, I clean, I sew. Accounts have to be paid,
            And Mother's so exact!
            Not that she needs be so tight-fisted, though, in fact!
            Where others spend a groat, we could afford far
               more—
            My father left us well provided for;
            A cottage and a garden near the town.
            But hours are still and days grown wan and plain.
            My brother's gone—
            A soldier. And my sister died.

---

[5] Gretchen is given her full name of Margarete in some scenes.   195

> In caring for her I was sorely tried,
> Yet I would undergo the agony again,
> I loved the child so much.   (*Garden*)

Much of Gretchen's story is told obliquely: the impersonal narrative style of balladry is taken over for stage use. Thus, her song at the spinning-wheel is presented ostensibly as a ballad she sings while working—it is only by implication we realise that it describes her own state of mind:

> My peace is gone,
> My heart is sore,
> I'll find it never,
> Nevermore.
>
> My spirit yearns
> To have him here,
> To clasp him to me
> And hold him near.
>
> To kiss him here
> With longing breath
> And in his kisses
> Greet my death.   (*Gretchen's Room*)

Even the crisis of her pregnancy is first announced to us in this way. Gretchen and her friend Lieschen discuss the fate of another girl, Barbara, yet since the story of a rich seducer was so common a theme in both ballads and *Sturm und Drang* drama, Goethe is able to make the slightest hint of Gretchen's predicament intelligible to the audience and, by so doing, avoids stressing the sordid particularity of the circumstance:

Lieschen: Haven't you heard about Barbara, now?
Gretchen: Nothing at all. But, then, I don't go out.
Lieschen: Sybil told me—there's no doubt.
    Her head's been turned and her pride must bow.
    What respectability!
Gretchen: Why?

Lieschen: It stinks!
            She feeds two now when she eats and drinks.
Gretchen: O God! . . . .
Lieschen: It's a fitting end to what began!
            Just think how long she doted on the man.
            How those dainty feet
            Led him a dance down the village street!
            And everywhere she was a queen,
            He brought her wine, he brought her cream,
            And she was the fairest ever seen!
            But yet so shameless that she'd take
            Every gift he cared to make.
            Too moist the lip, too hot the hands that close,
            Too soon the bloom forsakes the rose.   (*At the Fountain*)

Not till the end of the scene does Gretchen directly confess in her soliloquy that she, too, stands in Barbara's case.

Little circumstantial detail is given of either Gretchen's murdering the child, or of the death of her mother as a result of the sleeping-draught provided by Faust. To have provided such details would have again defeated Goethe's purpose of keeping the character blameless. The first reference Gretchen makes to the child's death is in the snatch of the ballad which Faust hears her sing from within the prison:

> My mother, the whore
> Who caused my death.
> My father, the knave
> Who ate my flesh.
> My sister gave
> My bones their grave
> Where cooling shadows play.
> My voice became the woodbird's lay:
> Fly away! Fly away!   (*Prison*)

It is clear she is speaking only partially of herself. The song refers to the events of *The Juniper Tree* legend in Grimm, and the ancient folk-tale of the stepmother who killed her stepson and fed him to his father at dinner (the child's bones being turned into a bird which sings this song), adds popular and classical overtones to Gretchen's tragedy. The dramatic method of the scene is similar to that of the fountain conversation, for again it is only later that Gretchen states the facts directly:

> My mother died by my own sin.
> I drowned my child.

Further details are only provided by disjointed phrases in her tormented wanderings. The death of her mother is recalled in a passage that suggests a nightmare:

> If only the mountain-side were passed!
> My mother sits there on a stone.
> Cold fingers snatch my tress!
> My mother sits there on a stone,
> Palsied with distress.
> She signs no sign, she makes no move,
> Heavy her head and sore.
> She slept so long, she woke no more.
> She slept that we might find our love
> In happier days long gone before.   (*Prison*)

The lines of Gretchen already quoted all occur in both the *Urfaust* and Part I (though there are slight modifications and the vision of her mother on the stone is in prose in the earlier version.) The introduction into Part I of the Witch's Kitchen, however, makes oblique poetic reference to Gretchen which throws important light on her symbolic function. Gretchen does not appear in the scene, but in the midst of the jabbering of Mephistopheles and the monkeys, Faust becomes aware of the magical appearance of a beautiful woman in the mirror. Immediately the tone of the verse changes—the woman is not Gretchen, but a reflection of the ideal beauty of which Gretchen is a particular manifestation. The change in the verse denotes that we are passing from realistic tomfoolery to idealised philosophy:

Mephisto (*nearing the fire*):   And what's this pot?
Male and Female Monkey: The stupid sot!
                        Don't know the pot!
                        Don't know the kettle!
Mephisto: Ill-mannered lot!
Monkey: Take this fly-swat
                        And sit there on the settle.
         (*He invites Mephistopheles to sit.*)
Faust (*who has meanwhile been standing before a mirror, sometimes approaching it, sometimes drawing back*):

                        What's here? What magical reflection
                        Of heaven's beauty gilds this glass?
                        O Love, endow me with your swiftest
                          wings to pass
                        Directly to her pure perfection.
                        Yet though I dare forsake my place
                        And come to her, the face is kissed
                        By lingering figments of eternal mist,
                        Which veil this loveliest form of
                        woman's grace.
                        Can it be true? Is she so fair?
                        Am I to find then in this woman's face
                        The quintessential breath of heaven's
                        air?
                        Is there such beauty on this earth?
                                  (*Witch's Kitchen*)

To the end of the scene Faust remains fascinated by her:

Faust: The mirror! Let me look in it once more.
            The woman's portrait was so fair!
Mephisto: No! No! You'll find perfection to adore
            In living flesh, not empty air.
                    (*softly*)
            With this drink in your veins, my boy,
            Each girl will be Helen of Troy!

In fact, the girl that Faust meets at the opening of the immediately following scene is Gretchen. Thus a connection between Helen and Gretchen is implied. The poetic overtones of the mirror sequence, and the reference to Helen, surround Gretchen before she enters and point directly to her eventual function of leading Faust to salvation. She has the immutable quality of womanhood (*das Ewig-Weibliche*) which is found also in Helen, in the *Mater Dolorosa* and also, in Goethe's other play, in Iphigenia.

The Characters of Faust and Mephistopheles

The Prologue in Heaven makes it clear that Mephistopheles' attempt to claim Faust's soul will fail. The Lord describes the Doctor as His servant, pointing out that though Faust follows the ways of goodness confusedly, he will eventually be led to light:

> For men must err while men still strive.

The tension of the play, therefore, does not depend on the outcome of the action but on the nature of it. The story is to lead to a conclusion which is contrary to that associated with the traditional Faust figure. How, we ask, is this to come about?

The avoidance of damnation can only be achieved if traditional religious attitudes and preconceptions are modified. The 'Devil' of the play cannot be the traditional figure of Absolute Evil, nor can Faust sell his soul to him for the traditional motive of material gain. The entire theological framework of the legend has to be reinterpreted and Goethe gives hint of this in Faust's opening words:

> I've sweated through philosophy,
> Jurisprudence, Medicine—
> Yes, and alas, Theology—
> Through and through and out and in!
> Poor fool! Poor disillusioned man,
> No whit more wise than you began!　　　(*Night*)

Even when Faust is deterred from suicide by the voices of

Easter Morning, it is clear that it is not Christian belief which
they reawaken in him, but memories of early life:

> Why seek me in the dust, you sound
> Of heaven's soft imperial strain?
> Pour forth your songs where gentler hearts are found.
> I hear your message run, but my belief is lame.
> Fond miracles were ever crowned
> As Faith's most favoured progeny.
> I do not dare aspire towards those spheres
> That ring such sacred prophesy.
> Accustomed, though, to hear their call from early years
> I now return to life . . . .
> . . . .
> This strain recalled to me the hectic hours of youth,
> The festival's untrammelled breath
> Which fed an infant soul. That memory—not truth
> Proclaimed on high—turns me from death.   (*Ibid.*)

In place of Christian faith, Faust shows at first a pantheistic
desire to be one with Nature—hence his summoning of the
Earth-Spirit. As we have seen from Schiller's essays, however,
eighteenth-century thought discerned an essential difference
between instinctive Nature and reflective Man—hence the
Earth-Spirit rejects Faust. The Doctor's quest then turns to
deeper investigations of human nature. He is aware, he tells
Wagner, of two souls in his breast: the first clings passionately
to earth, the second longs for higher realms. Yet the nature of
his spiritual ambition is strangely sensuous. It is the ambition
of a poet who longs to discover Truth through sensation not
abstraction. That customary theological speculation plays no
part in it, is revealed by his later words to Mephisto:

> If you devour this world, my care
> Will not be what lies over there!
> Let that come later. *This* earth's sun
> Shines as the only solace to my woe,
> From this earth's springs alone my pleasures flow.
> . . . .

> I have no appetite to hear
> If future hate and future love
> Persist in the eternal sphere,
> If hell's below or heaven above. (*The Study*)

Faust's ambition is to taste the whole of life and hence he gradually changes from a particular figure to a universal one. His adventures in Part II are an attempt to share the whole experience of the human race from the Creation (the discussion of Homunculus, Anaxagoras and Thales) through classical and medieval times to the Utopian world of the end. The desire for such experience is expressed in Part I, in words which remind us of lines from Keats's *Hyperion*. Keats speaks of the poet as one of those

> . . . to whom the miseries of the world
> Are misery, and will not let them rest.

Faust says to Mephistopheles:

> I said that I seek no felicity
> But sue for ecstasy, the cruellest of desires:
> Hate that is born of love and suffering which inspires.
> The quest for learning quenched within my mind,
> My heart henceforth repudiates no pain
> But gathers to it all that all mankind
> Must share. Their common lot be now my gain!
> My spirit shall reach out to height and depth,
> Their weal and woe be breath of my own breath,
> Till this mere self dilates, encompasses all men
> And perishes, at last, along with them. (*The Study*)

The combination of the sensuous with the intellectual makes Faust particularly susceptible to Mephisto's temptation. For Mephisto is the Spirit of Denial who seeks through men's appetites to mock idealism. As such, his character is smaller than that of Absolute Evil and, indeed, he is at pains to point out that he is only a part of Evil, adding that Evil, itself, is equally only a partial concept:

Faust: . . . .
Very well, who are you then?
Mephisto: A part of that which would
Eternally *will* Evil—and eternally *does* Good.
Faust: And must that riddle serve as explanation?
Mephisto: I am the Spirit of Negation!
And rightly so, for all that is created
Deserves to be disintegrated.
So it were better nothing should begin.
Thus, everything which you call sin,
Destruction, evil—all that's meant
By such words is my element.
Faust: You call yourself a part. You seem complete to me.
Mephisto: I spoke Truth unpretentiously.
It is mankind's habitual conceit
That he, poor idiot, is self-complete!
I'm part, then, of the part which preluded creation:
Part of primaeval darkness which gave light gestation.
Proud light! That now presumes to claim the place
Of Mother Darkness, and contests her space.
Strive though it may, it cannot win that fight,
For Substance has imprisoned Light.
Light streams from Substance, Substance shows it fair,
And Substance' barriers mark its course.
I trust, then, Light, together with its source
Will very shortly vanish in thin air!   (*Ibid.*)

Mephisto's aim is to delight Faust's senses so that his spiritual ambition is reduced to animal contentment—so that, in fact, he ceases to be Man. It is because Faust is confident that this can never happen that he concludes the wager:

Faust: If ever I should lie content in slothful ease,
At that point you may name me damned.
If flattery can cozen me
To thinking I am reconciled
To my own state, if I'm beguiled
By your delights—then let that be
My final day. So I demand
The wager then.

203

Mephisto:	Agreed!
Faust:	I give my hand.

If to some transient hour I cry
'Perfection's here! Suspend your flight!'
Cast me in chains and know that I
Walk willingly in Death's deep night.
Let funeral bells unfold their chime,
Your service ended, you be free.
Then let there be an end to time,
To clocks, to hour-hands, hours and me.   (*Ibid.*)

Yet the scene *Wood and Cave* indicates that though Faust will not succumb to Mephistopheles, he cannot do without him. The very pursuit of Ideals involves within itself the process of Denial. Faust thanks the Sublime Spirit of Nature for the gift of his companion: the opportunity to taste so much of life through Mephistopheles' assistance is like a gift from the Gods, but equally 'divine' is the rejection of each particular experience in the name of seeking Ultimate Experience:

O now I feel that man will never find
Perfection. You afforded me this bliss
Which brings me ever nearer to the Gods,
And gave me this companion without whom
I cannot live. Though insolent and cold,
And able to degrade me from myself,
Turning your gifts to nothing in a breath,
Yet still he fans wild fire within my heart
That longs to hold the beauty I have seen.
I tumble from desire into content
And in content still languish for desire.
                    (*Wood and Cave*)

Mephistopheles' fanning of the fires in Faust's heart reaches its supreme point in Part I in the visit to the *Walpurgisnacht* (St. Walpurgis' Night, the Witches' Sabbath) on the Brocken. An impressive and balletic moment in the drama it represents the crude, yet bustling and vital, existence in which Mephisto delights:

Chorus of Witches:
> The witches to the Brocken stream,
> Stubble's yellow, corn is green.
> The motley pack is gathered here
> And Urian sits enthroned as Peer!
> We clamber over fells and brinks,
> The witches fart, the he-goat stinks.

How well such scenes in Goethe's drama can be turned into cinema is shown by the Gustaf Gründgen film of *Faust*. Here the proceedings were given the entirely appropriate overtones of Bavarian Carnival, with its streamers, superficial gaiety and inward emptiness. At the climax of Gründgen's staging of the scene the mushroom cloud of the Hydrogen Bomb rose ominously above the dancers. This is in accord with Faust's own reaction: he turns his mind from the revelry in disgust, seeing the vision of Gretchen near to death, and round her neck:

> A lace of scarlet was displayed,
> As narrow as the razor's blade.

Though Mephisto's intention in taking Faust to the Brocken is to make him forget Gretchen, it has the opposite effect. He comes to see her plight more clearly, and in the ensuing *Dark Day* scene bitterly curses Mephisto for his part in her tragedy. Yet, as Mephisto coldly observes 'She is not the first'. The search for contentment leads all men, as it leads Faust, to ruthlessness. (The same lesson is shown in the Philemon and Baucis episodes of Part II.) Faust could never have been content married to Gretchen, any more than Goethe could have been with Friederike Brion. What finally 'saves' his soul is not Gretchen, but what Gretchen stands for, the perfection he was seeking in his heart.

Ultimately no particular manifestation of the Ideal will satisfy Faust. In this connection Bielschowsky's[6] observation that

[6] Albert Bielschowsky, *Life of Goethe* (translated by William Cooper). G. P. Putnam's Sons, New York and London. The Knickerbock Press, 1908, vol. III, p. 347.

Faust's dying words are a foretaste of contentment, not an emphatic statement of present enjoyment, is pertinent. True contentment remains only a theoretical possibility to the end:

And here, within, a land of paradise!
Beyond its rim the ocean tumults rise
And as they gnash in anger, men unite,
Sealing the gaping ravage of their spite.
Yes! I surrender heart and soul to this,
This final reach of wisdom's sway.
Life and the rich reward of freedom's bliss
Must be fought for day by day.
Both child and man, old age itself shall dwell
In freedom here, ringed round from danger's hell.
What would I give to see, to stand
With these free people on their own free land!
Why, then, I would command the transient hour
'Perfection's here, suspend your flight!'
The traces of my earthly power
Shall glimmer through eternal night.
Foretasting such felicity, I call
This present hour the apogee of all.

(Great Courtyard of the Palace)

The first production of *Faust, Part I* was a Court Theatre performance of certain scenes at Schloss Monbijou, the home of Duke Karl of Mecklenburg, on 24 May 1819. The cast was partly amateur, partly professional. In the two study scenes, Pius Alexander-Wolff played Faust (having already studied the part under Goethe, for a projected performance at Weimar which did not take place) and the Duke of Mecklenburg played Mephisto. The setting used for these scenes was as remarkable as the occasion itself, since it was the first time that a box-set had been used in Germany. Count Brühl, the director, entered into lengthy correspondence with Goethe concerning the problems of his task. In particular the appearance of the Earth-Spirit was discussed. Goethe had made a sketch of the Spirit and had intended attributing to him the features of Jupiter (a bust of Jupiter had, inded, been used at rehearsals in Weimar.) In Brühl's production, however, a bust of Goethe was placed outside the window of Faust's study—the head being of enormous proportions—and suitably lit at the appropriate moment. Goethe was apparently flattered.

Other episodes in the play were presented operatically, the roles being taken by opera singers from Berlin, and the music specially composed by Prince Anton Radziwill. The entire performance was given again in the presence of Frederick the Great a year later. On this occasion the scenes in Auerbach's Cellar and Gretchen's room were added—a box-set again being used for the Gretchen scene, though the employment of such settings did not become widespread in Germany until much later.

The first full production of Part I took place nine years later (1829) in Brunswick, subsequent performances being given in Dresden, Leipzig and Frankfurt. On the occasion of Goethe's eightieth birthday it was eventually staged at Weimar. Subsequently it has become one of the most frequently performed of all German classics, though it has not yet succeeded in finding the same popularity in the Anglo-Saxon theatre. This is partly, perhaps, due to the unfortunate nature of the early adaptations. In 1825 it was presented at Drury Lane by George Soames as a melodrama with the accompaniment of fireworks. In 1885 came W. G. Wills's travesty of the text with Irving as Mephistopheles at the Lyceum. Neither production can be said to have served Goethe even remotely well. In the twentieth century more serious attempts have been made to come near to the original text. A condensation of Parts I and II was presented at the Cambridge Festival Theatre in 1935 by Graham and Tristan Rawson. In 1949, as part of the celebrations for the bi-centenary of Goethe's birth, the B.B.C. serialised both parts in a translation for radio made by Louis MacNiece and E. L. Stahl. In the same year Part I was performed in Regent's Park and Gustaf Gründgen's memorable German production was seen at the Edinburgh Festival.

Faust is an unconventional drama, but Part I is both theatrically viable and splendidly spectacular. In writing it Goethe asked for little that could not be provided by the stages of his time. As always he was particularly conscious of lighting effects, as such scene titles as 'Night' and 'Dark day' demonstrate. Even the wine which turns into fire in the drinking scene was a possible illusion. Most eighteenth-century theatres were fitted with trap-doors in which powder could be pre-set near a constantly burning flame. A blow pipe was then used by a stage-hand to direct the flame to the powder at the right moment. The transformation of the poodle into Mephisto (so graphically described in the verse) is accompanied by clouds of misty smoke which again would have presented no great difficulties in realisation. In most modern productions the dog itself is left to the audience's imagination and, remembering the performance of *The Wood near Bondy*, we may safely assume that Goethe would have wished it to be so, although a contemporary illustration of the production of *Wallenstein's Camp* at Weimar seems to imply the presence of two dogs on the stage. Possibly, however, this is an artist's embellishment rather than a realistic reproduction of what occurred on stage.

More than any of his dramas, *Faust* reveals the breadth and uniqueness of Goethe's mind. For this reason even Part II will no doubt continue to claim the attention of directors. However eccentric its demands, it is the reflection of one of the greatest minds that ever lived and, what is more, of a mind which had long been occupied with practical theatre. If it were not for Goethe's years as Director of the Court Theatre, it would be easier to dismiss Part II as the unrealisable vision of a poet. The fact that it was not written for the stage is not entirely relevant, as the example of Ibsen's similar pieces, *Brand* and *Peer Gynt*, reminds us. In such cases the dramatic quality of the poet's mind is more significant than his immediate intention. Furthermore, in Goethe's case, we know that in his early plays, such as *Partners in Guilt* and *A Lover's Humour*, he had shown himself a master of conventional dramatic form. Such early work, however, remains slight. The mature poet needed a more personal and original style of theatre.

Despite its influence on Ibsen and the English Romantics, therefore, *Faust* cannot be considered as a model which other dramatists can successfully copy. Like *The Tempest* and Ibsen's *When We Dead Awaken* it is a form of drama uniquely suited to the mind which conceived it.

In some sense all Goethe's great dramas are of this kind, yet their relationship to each other, and to the plays of Schiller, teaches us much of the essential and abiding nature of theatre. The transition from *Sturm und Drang* to Classicism is of more than historical interest. It illustrates one facet of the continuing struggle within the mind of any artist between inspiration and expression, freedom and form. As we have seen, it is false to imagine that *Faust, Iphigenia, Mary Stuart* and *Tell* are totally different from *Götz* and *The Robbers*. The same themes of *Sturm und Drang* idealism appear in them all. In *Faust*, indeed, even the *Sturm und Drang* expression of the earlier written scenes is left intact in the final version. But a re-shaping of such elements is discernible in the later works: a clarity and simplicity of expression and action which arises from discipline of form. The popularity of the *Sturm und Drang* plays in recent years reminds us how near the 'sixties and seventies' of our time are to the thought of the young Schiller and the young Goethe. It is not, perhaps, inconceivable that our own drama, too, may weary of its delight in 'lawlessness' and its violent reaction against the artificiality of the 'well-made play'. It will not regress to the old forms it has rejected, but in its search for new disciplines may find the theatre of Goethe and Schiller has much to teach. The strength of their theatre was the variety of its experiments in both writing and staging, yet the subjection of such experiments to the laws of art. Although a theatre in which the spoken word was paramount, it also paid great attention to the visual. It aspired in many ways towards the Total Work of Art envisaged by Wagner, in which words, music, mime and scenery worked in harmony towards a single end. Its influence on the subsequent history of the European stage was extensive: the theatre of the Duke of Meiningen extended and expanded Goethe's theories of staging, the scope of *Faust* has inspired some of the best work of a director like Reinhardt and a designer like Teo Otto. The concept of theatre in Germany as an educational force which deserves adequate financial backing from the State, together with such things as pensions for actors, owes much to the work of Goethe and Schiller. Yet their greatest theatrical significance lay, of course, in the plays themselves. In *Faust, Tasso, Iphigenia, Wallenstein, Mary Stuart* and *Tell* the stages of the world were enriched by a poetry which no other nation could equal in the eighteenth century. In England dramatic verse still laboured under the yoke of stale Shakespearian imitation. In Germany the glories of Shakespearian verse were born again in a new language which was as fresh and natural as that which he had used. With it went the strength of Schiller's philosophy and flair for theatrical effects, the richness of Goethe's personal experience and the subtlety of both poets (each in his own way) to explore character on the stage.

Select Bibliography

Boyd, J.: *Goethe's Iphigenie auf Tauris*, Oxford, 1942.
  Detailed analysis of play, throwing useful light on Weimar Classicism.
Bruford, W. H.: *Theatre, Drama and Audience in Goethe's Germany*, London, 1950.
  Valuable survey of German theatre 1700–1832, containing lists of performances and presenting the social background and ideas of the time.
Garland, H. B.: *Schiller*, London, 1949.
  Good general criticism of plays, with biographical details.
Garland, H. B.: *Schiller the Dramatic Writer*, Oxford, 1969.
  Particularly useful to the study of the language of Schiller's plays.
Gillies, A.: *Goethe's Faust, an Interpretation*, Oxford, 1957
  Scene by scene analysis of both parts. Recommended as introduction to the vast literature on the subject.
Gray, Ronald: *Goethe. A critical Introduction*, Cambridge, 1967.
  Excellent introduction to Goethe's works with chapters on the plays.
Kindermann, Heinz: *Theatergeschichte Europas*, Salzburg, vol. IV, 1961; vol. V, 1962.
  Particularly recommended for theatrical history of Weimar and its plays. Earlier and later volumes also contain important references to Goethe and Schiller.
Mainland, W. F.: *Schiller and the Changing Past*, London, 1957.
  Stimulating discussion of characters and motivation in Schiller's major plays.

Peacock, Ronald: *Goethe's Major Plays*, Manchester, 1959.
A sensitive and important study of Goethe's concept of drama.
Stahl, E. L.: *Friedrich Schiller's Drama, Theory and Practice*, Oxford, 1954.
Detailed discussion of Schiller's theory and practice, especially relevant to his concept of the hero's guilt and suffering.

BIBLIOGRAPHY

Bielschowsky, Albert: *Life of Goethe*, New York and London, 1908.
Carlyle, Thomas: *The Life of Friedrich Schiller*, London, 1845.
Devrient, E.: *Geschichte der deutschen Schauspielkunst*. ed. W. Stuhlfeld. Berlin & Zürich. 1929.
Eliot, T. S.: *Goethe as the Sage* (in *On Poetry and Poets*), London, 1957.
Fairley, Barker: *Goethe as revealed in his poetry*, London, 1932.
Fairley, Barker: *A Study of Goethe*, Oxford, 1947.
Fairley, Barker: *Goethe's Faust. Six Essays*, Oxford, 1953.
Flemming, Willi: *Goethe und das Theater seiner Zeit*, Stuttgart, 1968.
Friedenthal, R.: *Goethe: his Life and Times*, London, 1965.
Genast, Eduard: *Aus Weimars klassischer und nachklassischer Zeit, Erinnerungen eines alten Schauspielers*, Ed. R. Kohlrausch, 4th edn, Stuttgart, 1905.
Gräf, Hans Gerhard and Leitzmann, Albert: *Der Briefwechsel zwischen Schiller und Goethe*, Frankfurt-am-Main, 1964.
Hatfield, H. C.: *Goethe: a Critical Introduction*, Cambridge, Mass., 1964.
Huesmann, Heinrich: *Shakespeare-Inszenierungen unter Goethe in Weimar*, Vienna, 1968.
Iffland, A. W.: *Ueber meine theatralische Laufbahn*, Ed. H. Holstein, Heilbronn, 1886, Deutsche Literaturdenkmale, no. 24.
Jagemann, Karoline: *Erinnerungen*, Ed. E. v. Bamberg, Dresden, 1926.
Kindermann, Heinz: *Theatergeschichte der Goethezeit*, Vienna, 1948.
Kindermann, Heinz: *Die Entwicklung der Sturm- und Drangbewegung*, Vienna. 1925.
Kerry, S. S.: *Schiller's Writings on Aesthetics*, Manchester, 1961.
Knudsen, H.: *Goethes Welt des Theaters*, Berlin, 1949.

Köster, Albert: *Schiller als Dramaturg*, Berlin, 1891.

Lewes, G. H.: *The Life and Works of Goethe*, London, 1885; Everyman Library, 1908.

Lukács, G.: *Goethe and his Age* (translated by Robert Anchor), London, 1968.

McNeile-Dixon, W.: *Tragedy*, London, 1924.

Miller, R. D.: *Schiller and the Ideal of Freedom*, Oxford, 2nd edn, 1970.

Moore, W. G.: *A new reading of Wilhelm Tell* (in *German Studies*), Oxford, 1938.

Pascal, Roy: *Shakespeare in Germany 1740–1815*, Cambridge, 1937.

Pasqué, Ernst: *Goethes Theaterleitung in Weimar*. Leipzig. 1863.

Peacock, Ronald: *Goethe's Version of Poetic Drama* (in *The Poet in the Theatre*), 2nd edn, London, 1960.

Robertson, J. G.: *Lessing's Dramatic Theory, being an Introduction to and Commentary on his Hamburgische Dramaturgie*, Cambridge, 1939.

Robertson, J. G.: *Schiller after a Century*, Edinburgh, 1905.

Rose, William: (Editor) *Essays on Goethe*, London, 1949.

Santayana, George: *Three Philosophical Poets*. Harvard, 1910.

Sichardt, Gisela: *Das Weimarer Liebhabertheater unter Goethes Leitung*, Weimar, 1957.

Stahl, E. L.: *Shakespeare und das deutsche Theater*, Stuttgart, 1947.

Stahl, E. L.: *Goethe's Iphigenie auf Tauris*, London, 1961.

Staiger, Emil: *Goethe*, Zürich, 1957–9.

Staiger, Emil: *Friedrich Schiller*, Zürich, 1967.

Steiner, George: *The Death of Tragedy*, London, 1961.

Wiese, Benno von: *Deutsche Dramaturgie vom Barock bis zur Klassik*, Tübingen, 1956.

Wilkinson, E. and Willoughby, L. A.: *Goethe Poet and Thinker*, London, 1962.

Index

216